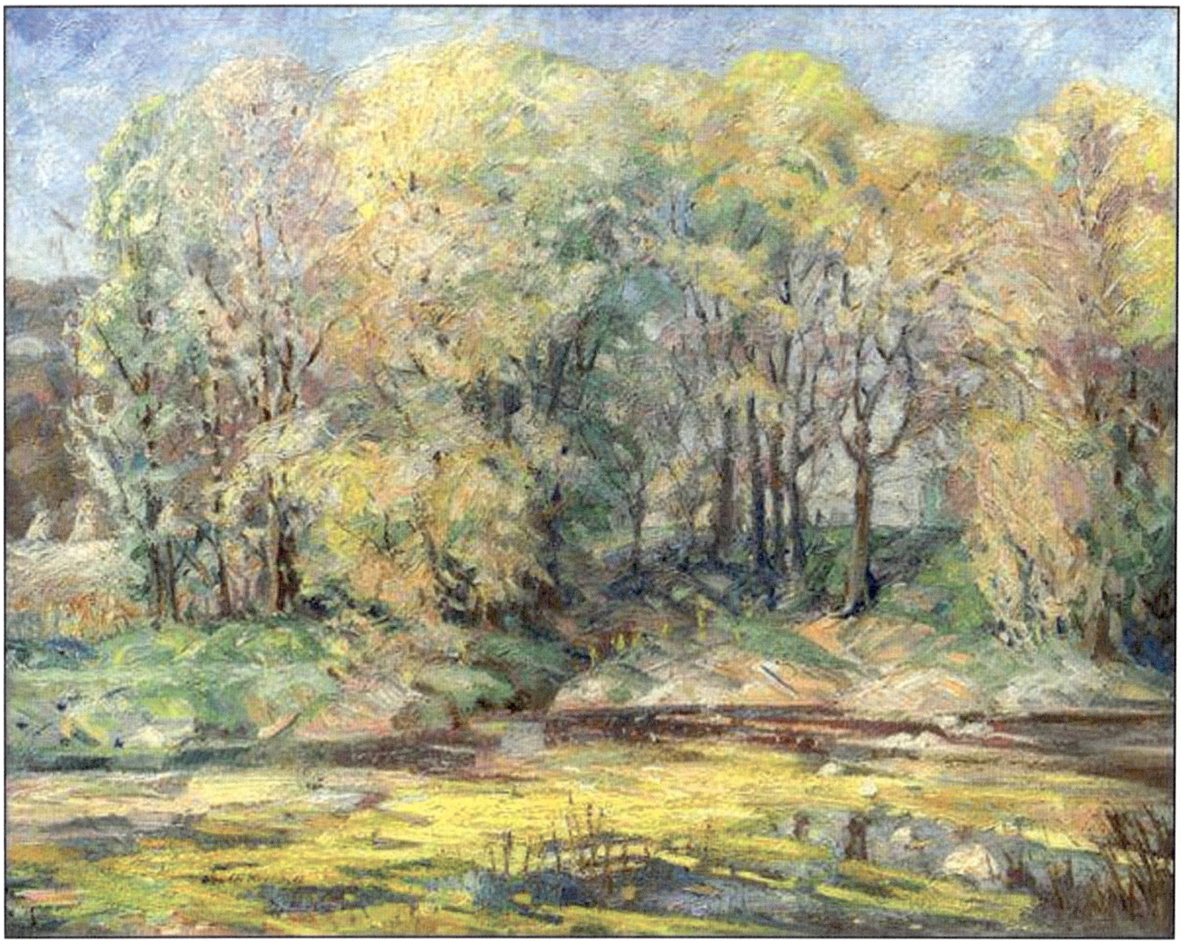

Golden Yellow Landscape, Albert H. Krehbiel, ca. 1930, 27 x 34, oil on canvas.

Albert Henry Krehbiel (1873-1945): American Impressionist, Muralist and Art Educator
by Donald T. Ryan, Jr.

Website: www.KrehbielArt.com

All works by Albert H. Krehbiel (other than mural works) and by Dulah Marie Evans (Krehbiel) as well as archival photographs and items presented in this publication are held in the collection of the Krehbiel Corporation as of the date of this printing unless otherwise stated.

The dimensions of all works in this publication other than murals are provided in inches.

"If someone could splash a rainbow and catch the shower of colors on canvas, that was Krehbiel. His pictures will long be remembered for their happy note, their impression of joy in nature, and the sheer beauty of their impetuous, irresponsible color."

-- **Eleanor Jewett, Art Critic, *Chicago Tribune*, July 15, 1945**

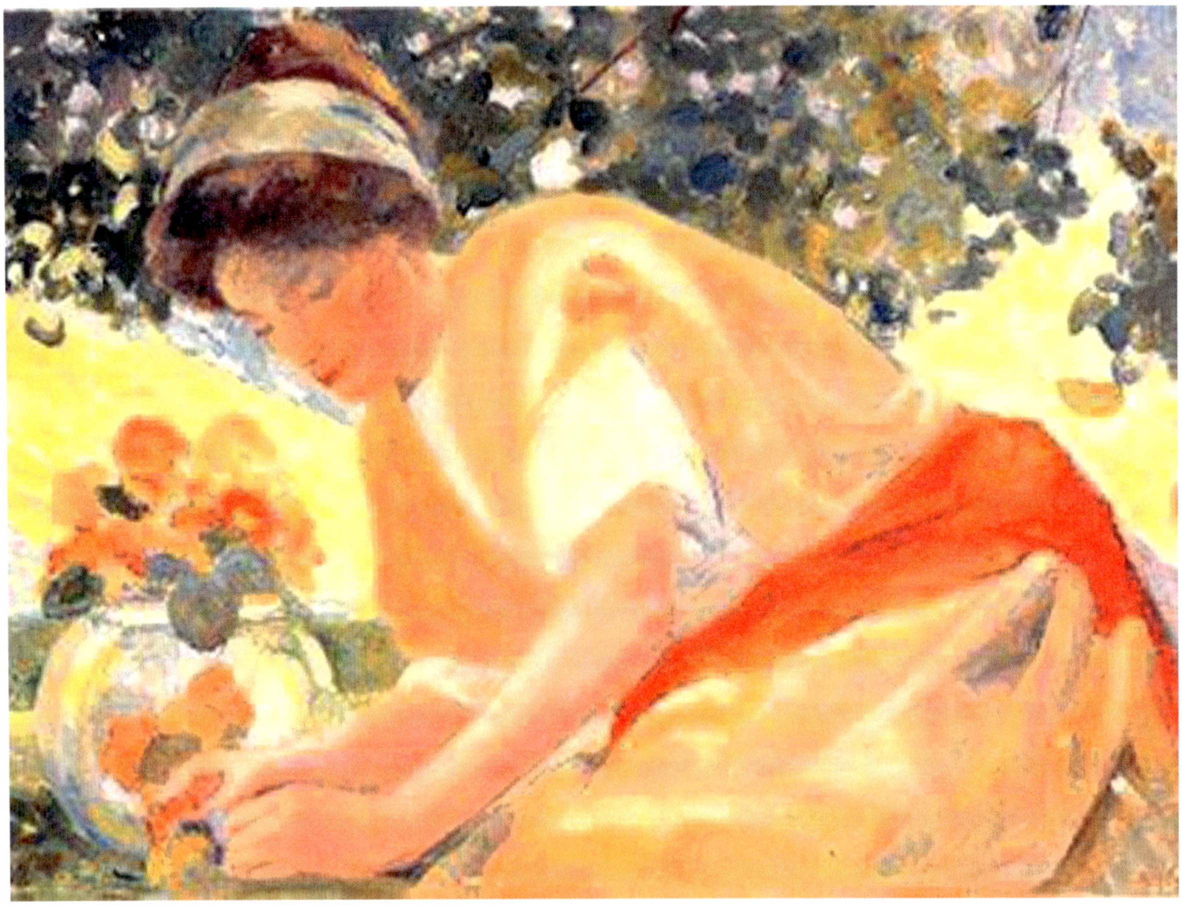

Lady and Her Bowl of Nasturtiums, Park Ridge, Illinois, ca. 1914, 22 x 30, oil on canvas.

Acknowledgements

Much of the text and theme of this account of Albert Krehbiel's life and works is derived from the following sources:

Albert Krehbiel: An American Impressionist, by Kim Coventry; Sonnenschien Gallery; Lake Forest College; Lake Forest, Illinois; 1989; 11 pp., ill.

Allegories of Justice, The Albert H. Krehbiel Murals in the Supreme Court Building of Illinois, cover article by Lizabeth (Betsy) Wilson; **Journal of the Illinois Historical Society**; ISSN 0019-2287; Spring 1984; pp. 2 - 13.

Krehbiel, Life and Works of an American Artist, by Robert Guinan; Regnery Gateway, Washington, D.C.; 1991; 33 pp., [66] pp. of plates: ill. (most color)

The authors of these sources deserve a great deal of the credit for this writing. Their diligent and exhaustive research and excellent artistic analysis helped to make this biography possible.

Special thanks and appreciation to Jane Meyer of J. Meyer Fine Art, Elburn, Illinois, for her continuous contribution in researching the extensive writings, letters, and archival material of Albert Henry Krehbiel.

Don Ryan

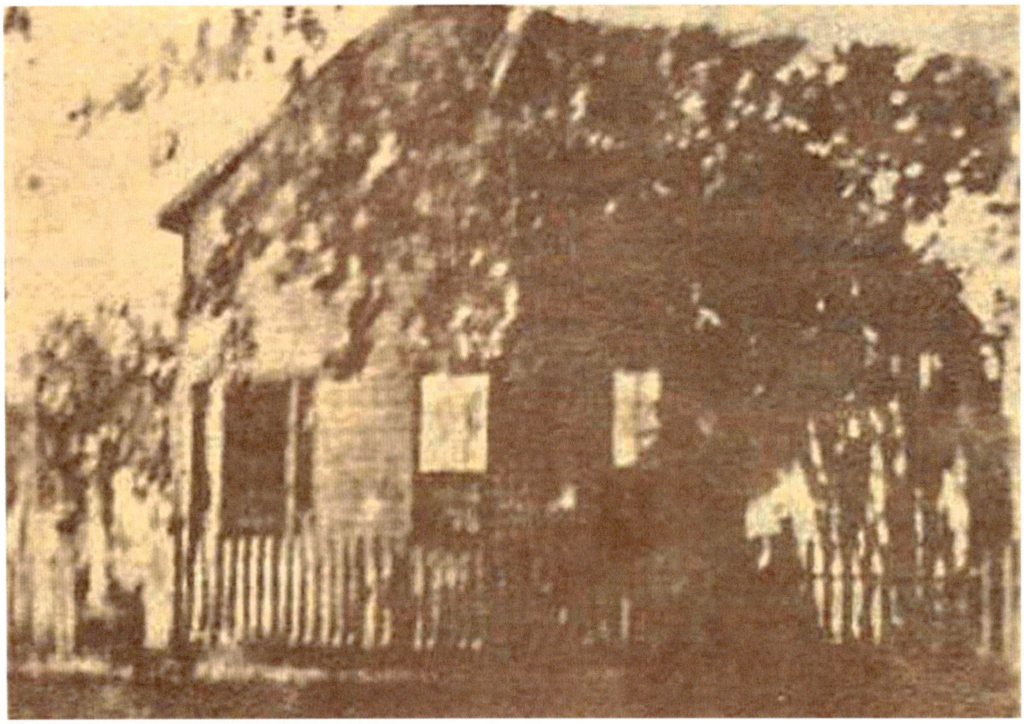

The Krehbiel family home in Denmark, Iowa, in 1867 - six years before Albert was born there in 1873.

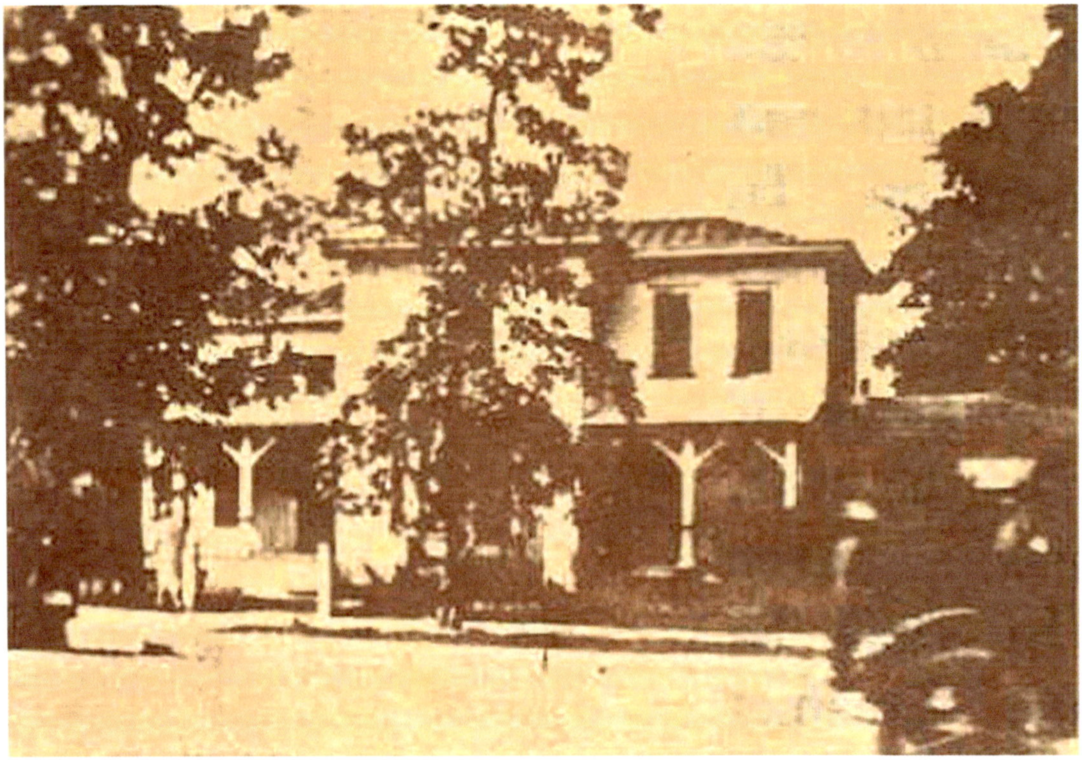

The Krehbiel family moved to Newton, Kansas, in 1879. The Krehbiel home in Newton, circa 1890.

Albert Henry Krehbiel

(1873-1945)

American Impressionist, Muralist and Art Educator

Table of Contents

Journal (from SMA)
Kr does not own
See if we get more

"Men cannot stop growing, nor [illegible] ew things merely in imitation of what has [illegible] t have its new tempo, its own plan and pat[illegible] ess itself soundly in the terms of that pattern and in [illegible] of that tempo."

Albert H. Krehbiel
Saugatuck, Michigan, 1930

The Early Years

Albert Henry Krehbiel, one of seven children, was born in Denmark, Iowa, on November 25th, 1873, to John Jacob and Anna Leisy Krehbiel. In 1879, he moved with his family to Newton, Kansas, where his father was a prominent Mennonite layman, prosperous carriage and buggy maker, and later a co-founder of Bethel College. At a very young age, Krehbiel expressed a desire to pursue drawing and painting. As a child, he had taken to painting the sides and wheels of the buggies made by his father's company and spent his school days drawing cartoons of his teachers and fellow students, much to the enjoyment of his peers and the consternation of his educators. 1

Krehbiel attended Bethel College in Newton for two years at the insistence of his practical minded father and, in 1895, he entered the School of Design and Painting in Topeka, Kansas *(see Fig. 1)*.

Fig. 1 Albert Krehbiel painting in watercolor at the School of Design and Painting, Topeka, Kansas, circa 1896.

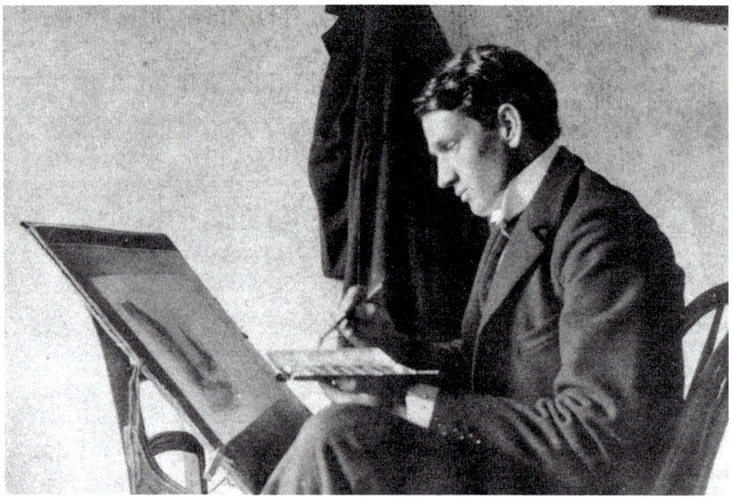

"European-trained George Stone conducted the art school assisted by his capable French wife, who inspired Krehbiel's love of the French language and people. Upon visiting the school on a lecture tour, Art Institute of Chicago Director William Merchant Richardson French discovered Krehbiel's talents and encouraged him to further pursue a career in art by enrolling at The Art Institute." 1 In a letter written May 14th, 1896, to his friend Sude (Herman Suderman, later his brother-in-law), Krehbiel wrote:

> ***" . . . I suppose you knew that I had returned*** *(to the family home in Newton)* ***and was serving my sentence in the shop. I am bound for Chicago in the fall. I am now turning out the necessary funds."*** 1

In the summer of 1898, Krehbiel made his way from Newton to Chicago by bicycle with his younger brother, Fred, and enrolled at The Art Institute for the fall semester. He labored for the next five years at The Art Institute as a student - three of them with painter and instructor of drawing, Frederick Richardson (1862-1937), and, in the fifth year, as a drawing instructor. "The academic curriculum at The Art Institute was based upon the strict French regime, with long hours devoted to working from the model as well as from casts of antique sculpture." [2] Among the many prizes and awards granted Krehbiel during these years at The Art Institute, he received an American Traveling Scholarship to study abroad in 1902.

"By 1903, Impressionism in Europe had run its course and, although it was not yet fully understood in America, French impressionist paintings had been entering American private collections and museums. Despite this, Krehbiel sought the rigorous training of a traditional art academy rather than joining the many American artists who continued the French tradition of studying impressionistic painting in the French countryside." [1] He headed for Paris to study for three years at the Academie Julian under Jean-Paul Laurens (1838-1921), one of the last great history painters.[1] Known primarily for his large historical paintings *(see Fig. 2)*, Laurens was also a muralist; in fact, he was considered a rival of the renowned Pierre Puvis de Chavannes (1824-1898). One of the most respected artists of his time, Laurens was revered by Auguste Rodin and later by French writers Charles Péguy and Andre Gide.

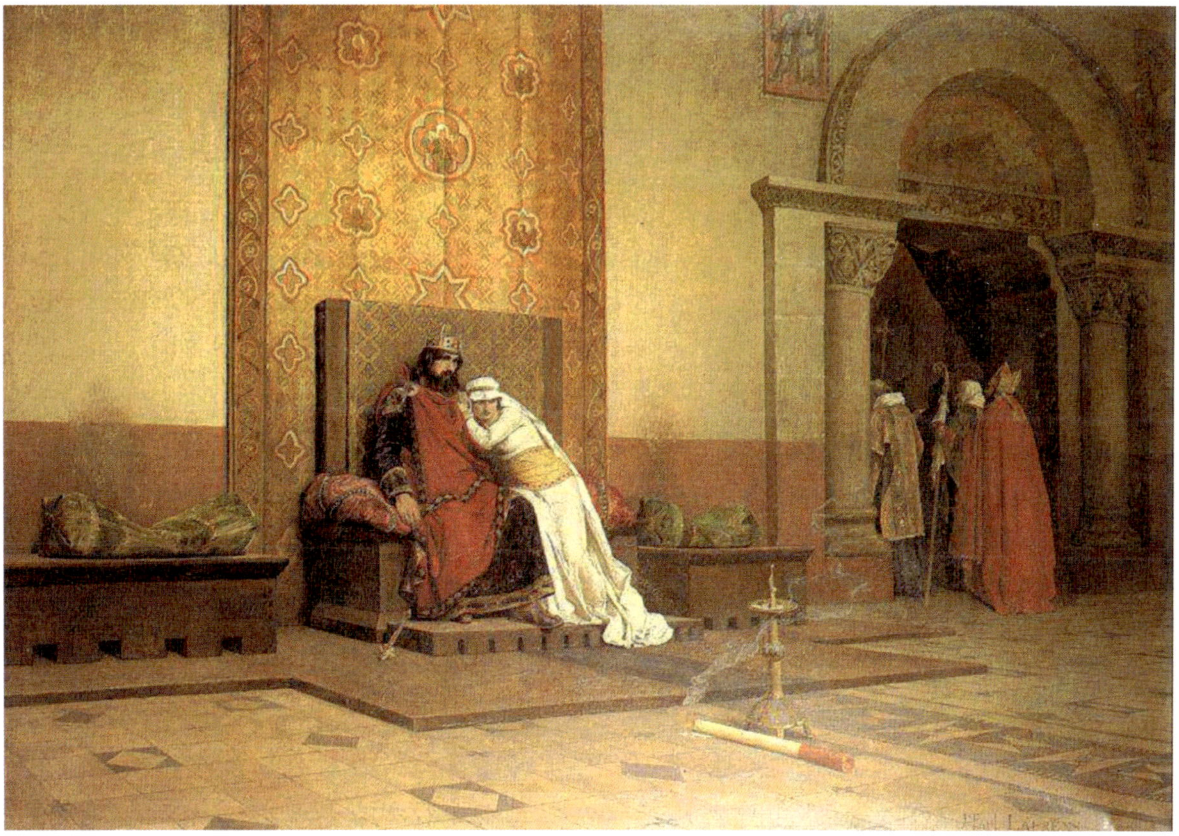

Fig. 2 *The Excommunication of Robert the Pious*, Jean-Paul Laurens, 1875, 51 1/4 x 85 3/4 (130 x 218 cm.), oil on canvas. Musée d'Orsay, Paris, France.

Krehbiel in Europe - His Studies and His Works

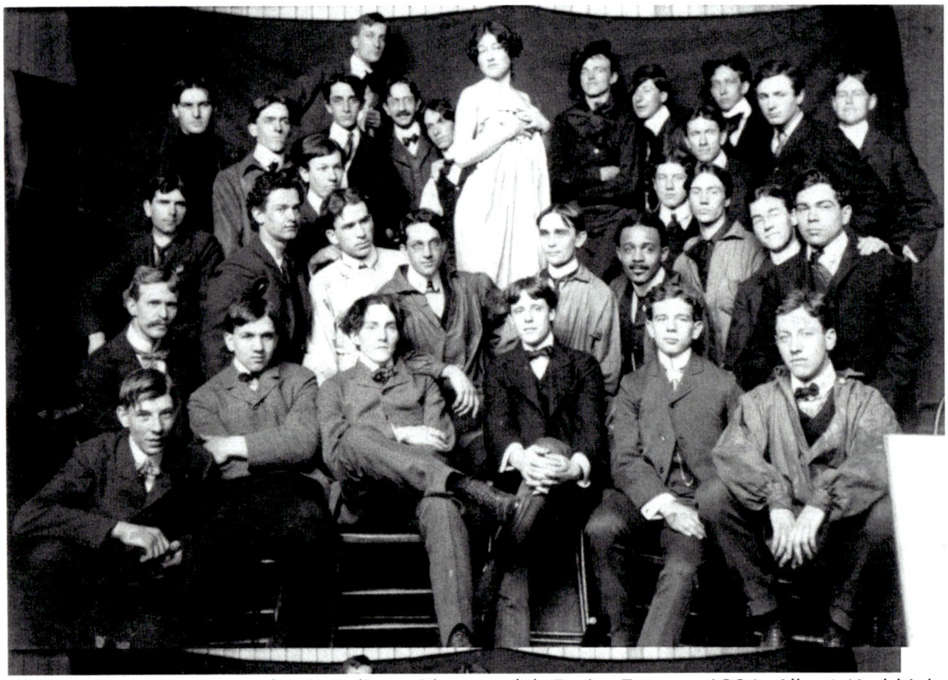

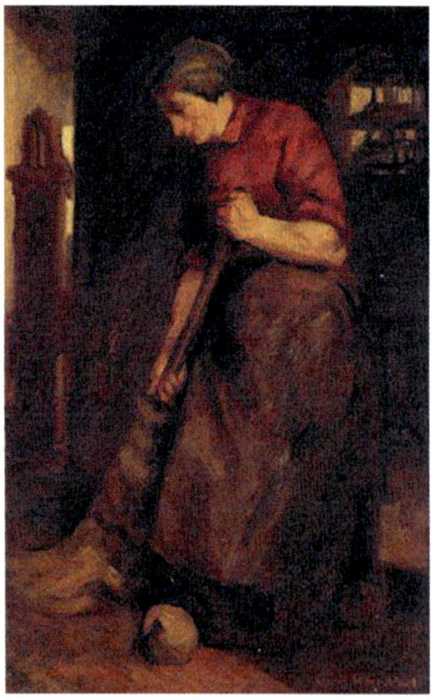

Above The class at Academie Julian with a model, Paris, France, 1904. Albert Krehbiel is the fourth student from the left in the second row.

Below and lower right Some of Krehbiel's charcoal sketches done both in his summer travels throughout Holland and France and as a student at Academie Julian, 1903-1906.
Top right *Woman Sweeping*, Paris, ca. 1904, 33 x 21, oil on canvas.

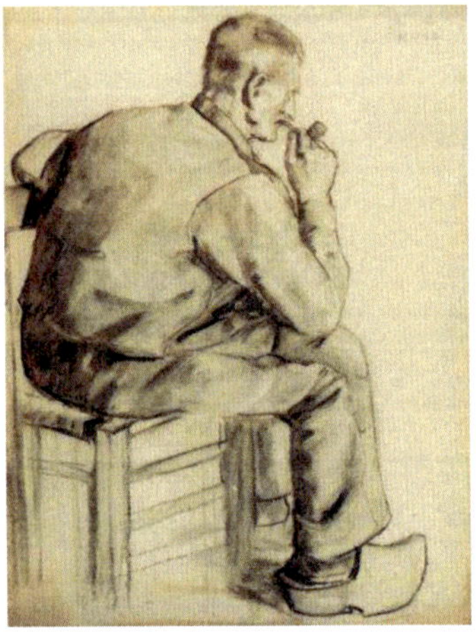

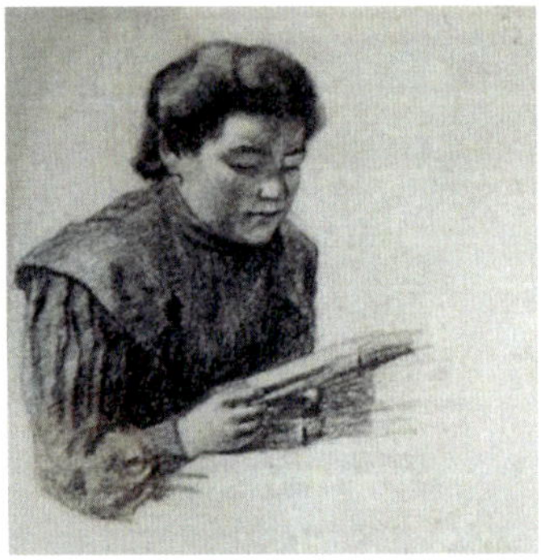

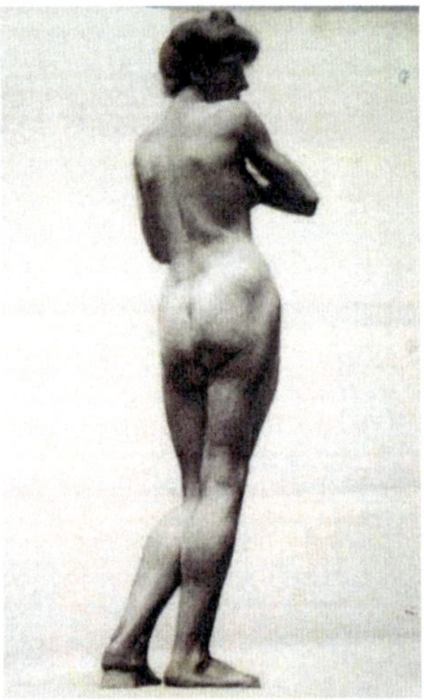

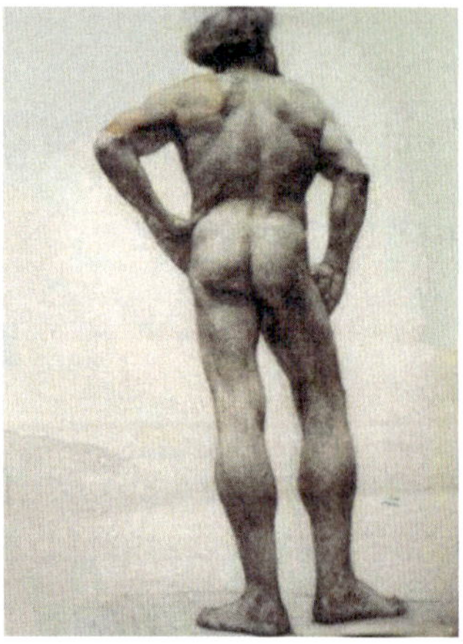

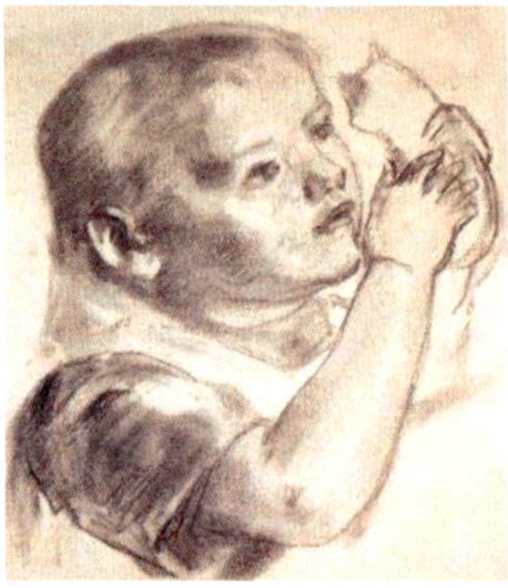

Krehbiel sailed for Europe on a steamer of the Holland-America Line and landed on July 23rd, 1903. His classes in Paris would not begin until October, so he settled in Laren, Holland, with the Dutch relatives of one of his fellow passengers and spent the next two months sketching and, at rare times, painting *(see Fig. 9 on page 5)* local citizens in their daily routine of work and at rest. Krehbiel would create many more such sketches in the following two years while on summer vacation from Academie Julian, traveling the countrysides of France and Holland - often accompanied by his friend, fellow Julian classmate, and later California impressionist, Joseph Raphael (1869-1950). *(See Figs. 3,4, and 5 and sketches on page 3.)* Krehbiel reproduced several of his sketches in oil on canvas when in Paris *(Figs. 6, 7, and 8)*.

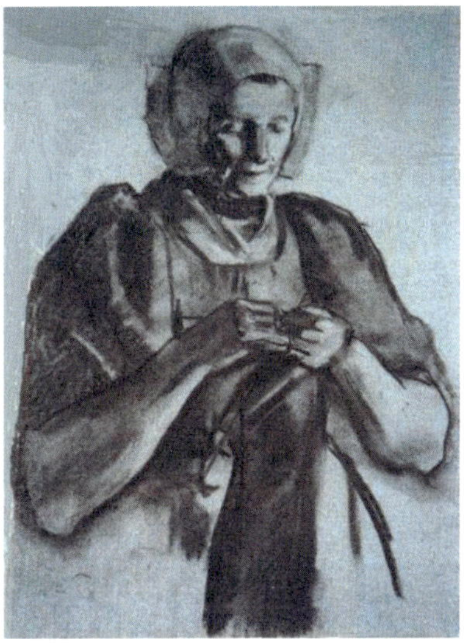

Fig. 3 Sketch for *Woman Knitting* (standing), Holland, ca. 1904, 19 x 12, charcoal on paper.

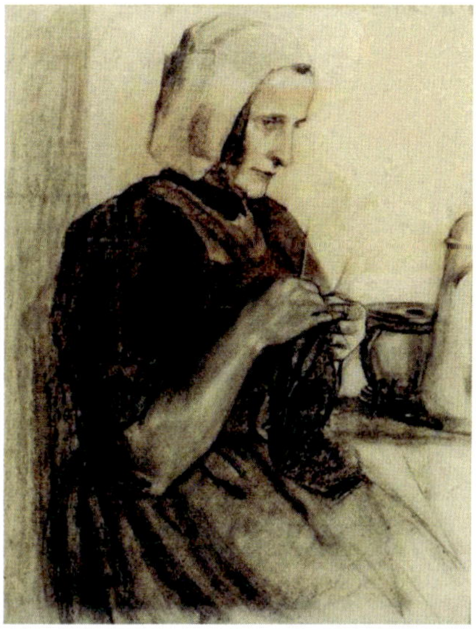

Fig. 4 Sketch for *Woman Knitting* (seated), Holland, ca. 1904, 24 x 19, charcoal on paper.

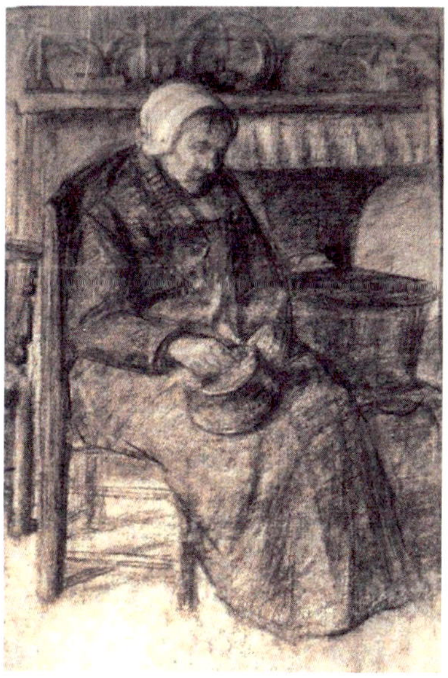

Fig. 5 Sketch for *Meditation,* Holland, ca. 1904, 25 x 17, charcoal on paper.

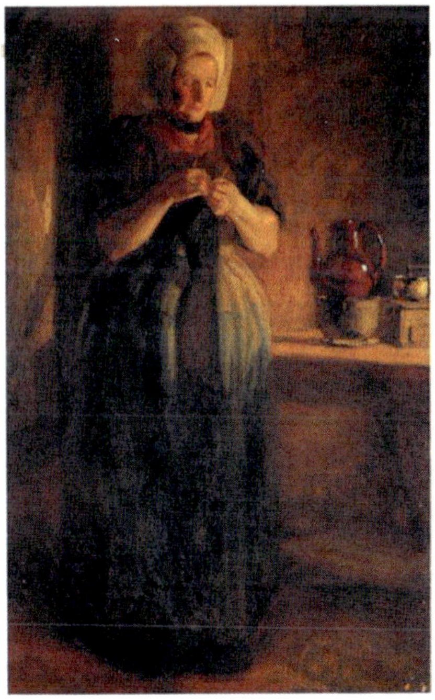

Fig. 6 *Woman Knitting* (standing), Paris, France, ca. 1904, 47 x 30, oil on canvas.

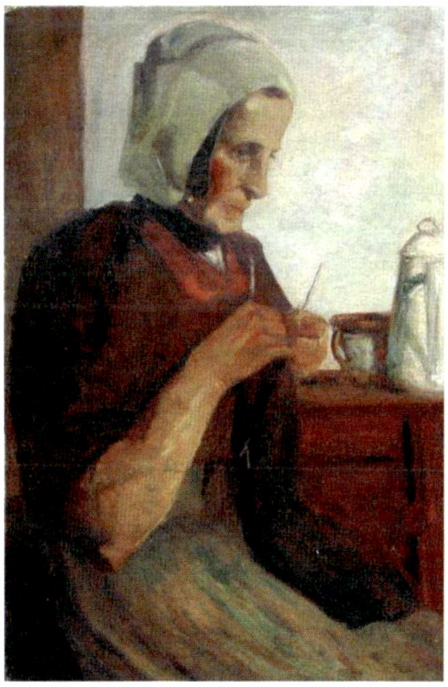

Fig. 7 *Woman Knitting* (seated), Paris, France, ca. 1904, 32 x 19, oil on canvas.

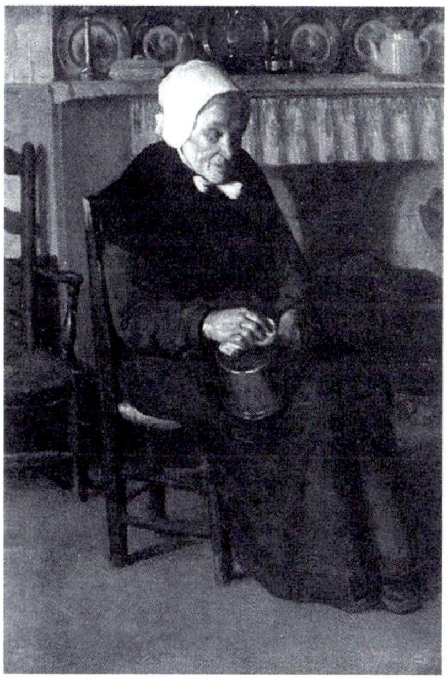

Fig. 8 *Meditation* (from black and white archive photo) , Paris, France, 1905, (size not known), oil on canvas.

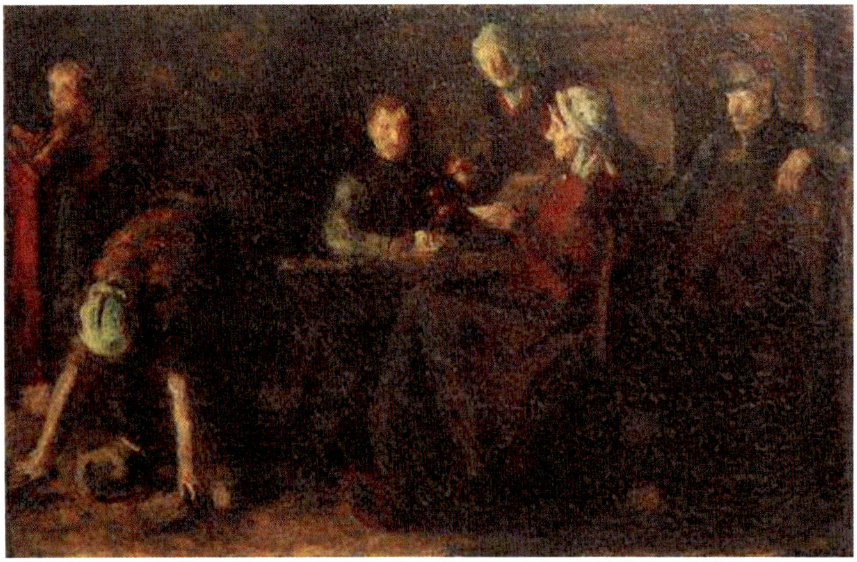

Fig. 9 *A Dutch Interior*, Laren, Holland, 1904, 10½ x 16, oil on board.

"Krehbiel wrote long personal letters during two periods of his life. The first occurred during his stay in Europe when he wrote to Dulah Marie Evans, his former classmate at The Art Institute and later his wife. These letters read much like a diary, recording his thoughts about the progress of his work as well as his impressions of Europe." 1 On September 14, 1903, Krehbiel wrote from Holland:

> ***"Last week I thought that I would have a painting to send you with Perret*** *(a traveling companion)* ***when he went over, but it is out of the question now. I'd worked for a week on an old man standing by a door looking at a couple of children . . . Just about noon the sun came out and made the canvas look so dingy that I took the pallet knife and scraped the whole blumin' lot out."*** 1

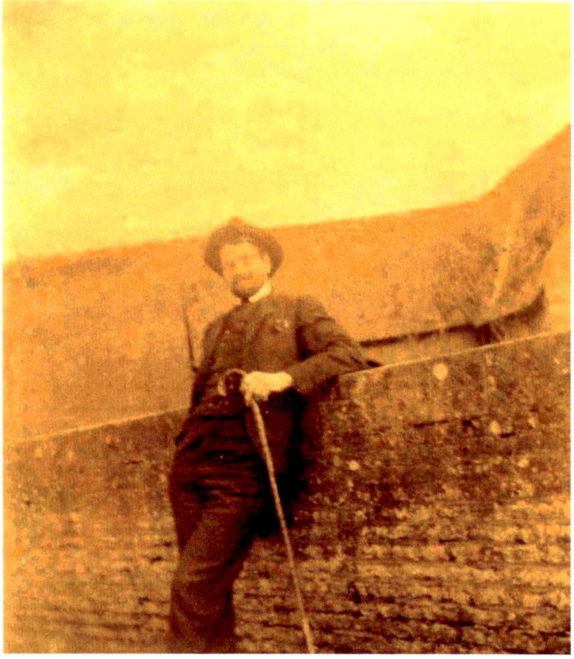

Fig. 10 Krehbiel in Muiden, Holland, July 20, 1904.

"Arriving in Paris at the end of September, Krehbiel began his studies at the Academie Julian on October 2nd. The curriculum at Academie Julian was centered on principles that had been espoused by Jacques Louis David (1748-1825). David's presence dominated French art from the age of Louis XVI through the periods of Jacobin and Napoleon, and his works epitomized the ideas of neoclassicism. Classical and biblical subjects became the only ones suitable for grand painting in France and, into the twentieth century, were the ones most likely to be accepted by the jury for the annual exhibitions at the prestigious Salon Des Artistes Francais (also known as the Paris Salon)." 2 In 1905, Krehbiel received the honor of having two of his neoclassical entries accepted for the exhibition. Also in 1905, two of his Dutch paintings were shown in the autumn exhibition at The American Art Association of Paris and one of them was sold for 100 francs (the other work is *Woman Sweeping,* page 3, top right).

Though Krehbiel had displayed a notable talent to paint under the rigid guidelines of French academic realism and neoclassicism, he pursued it without enthusiasm. Writing of a visit to the Louvre and a viewing of the *Tennis Court Oath* by Jacques-Louis David *(Fig. 11)*, he states:

> " . . . *(The work is done)* ***with no artistic expression whatsoever, merely mechanical and intellectual, . . . the Louvre is full of this sort of thing and lots of it. One wonders how the artist had the nerve to call it painting."*** 2

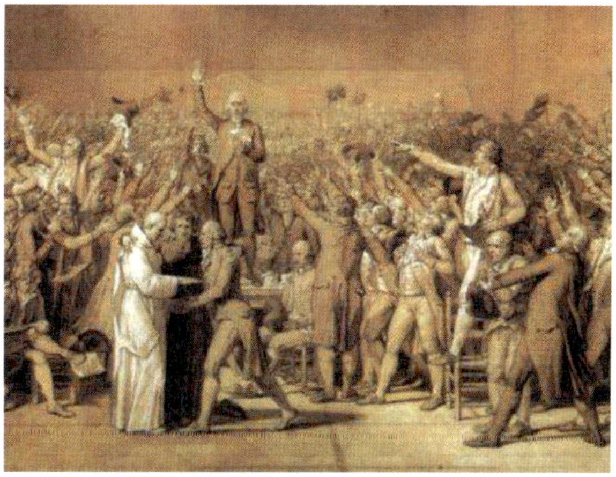

Fig. 11 *The Tennis Court Oath* (partial), Jacques-Louis David, 1789-92, 25 1/2 x 41 1/4 (65 x 105 cm), pen and bistre wash drawing. Musée du Louvre, Paris, France.

Krehbiel won four gold medals in competition while at Academie Julian *(Fig.12)* - the only American ever to have done so - as well as several other prizes and honors, including five cash prizes and permanent placement on the school wall of a painting on a biblical subject taken from the Book of Samuel.2 On February 9th, 1904, Krehbiel wrote to Dulah from his studio at No. 9 Rue Champagne, Paris, regarding being awarded a gold medal:

> ***" . . . My winning of the prize at Julian's last week seems to have given me some reputation. I am still receiving congratulations and everyone seems to think it such a feat that I'm beginning to wonder whether I'm not something after all."*** 1

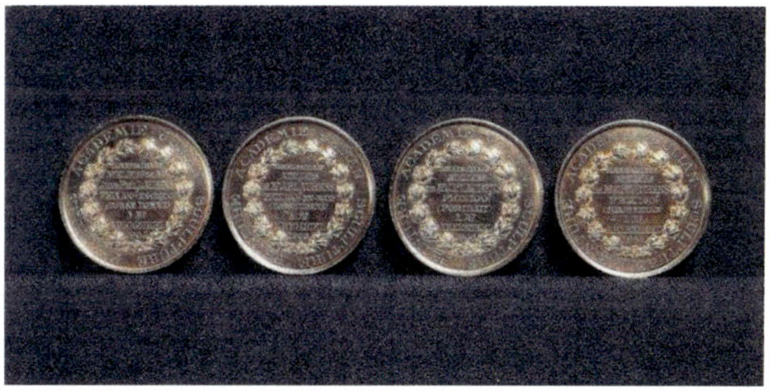

Fig. 12 Krehbiel's four gold medals won at Academie Julian, Paris, 1903-1906. Krehbiel Corporation collection.

In 1905, Krehbiel won the coveted Prix de Rome, which was given annually to the young painter who, in the eyes of the Academie, could produce the best composition in the prescribed manner of a Biblical or Classical subject.

"Krehbiel's classmates seem to have been more impressed with his awards than he was. When one of them sought his advice on how to go about winning a gold medal, he advised the man to concentrate on the development of his work and not on the winning of prizes." 2 His final attitude in speaking of the awards seems to be one of indifference, expressing that too much self-admiration would hinder his development as an artist. Regarding a medal awarded him in 1906, Krehbiel wrote in a letter home:

> ***" . . . It looks like the one from last year, with the exception of the date . . . the students crowded around me to handle the trophy, after which I dropped it into my pocket and went to work."*** 2

In the summer of 1906, Krehbiel's last year abroad, he made a walking and painting tour of Spain *(see Spanish Bullfight, Fig. 13)*, again traveling with friend and fellow student Joseph Raphael. Upon receiving special permission from Museo Del Prado in Madrid, Krehbiel spent three weeks making several miniature studies first hand of works done by Diego Velazquez (1599-1660) *(see Figs. 14 and 15)*. Nine of the studies were later shown at The Art Institute of Chicago's *Exhibition of Artists' Copies of Paintings by Old Masters* (July 26th to August 28th, 1910). In a letter to Dulah, Krehbiel wrote of his encounter with Velazquez:

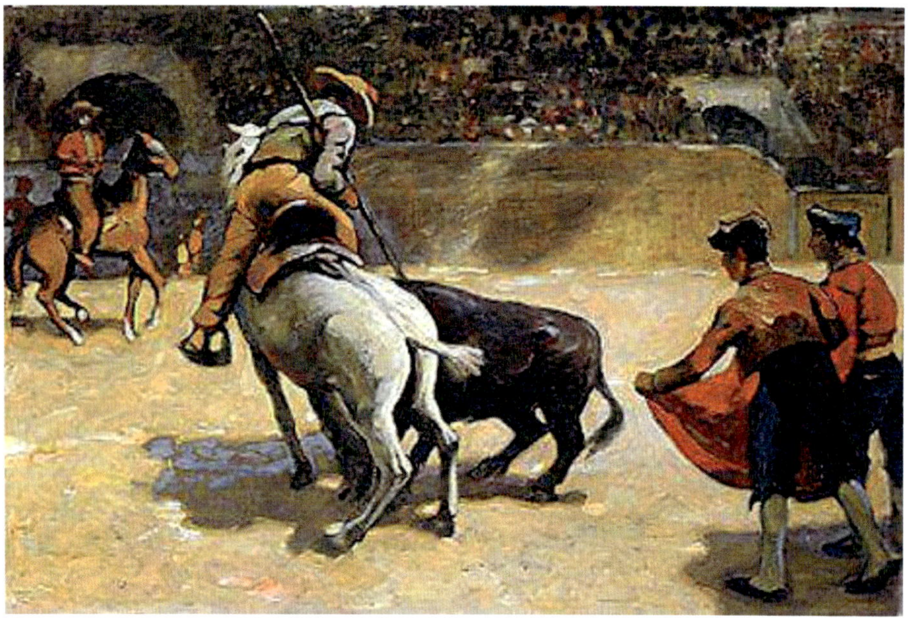

Fig. 13 *Spanish Bullfight,* Madrid, Spain, 1906, 25 x 36, oil on canvas. Collection of The Burlington Northern and Santa Fe Railway Company, Fort Worth, Texas.

> ***" . . . They seem so easily done . . . almost painting by accident . . .*** *(each figure)* ***seems to be breathing the air around him . . . the whole reveals itself to the mind as a good picture should, without any effort on the part of the beholder."*** [2]

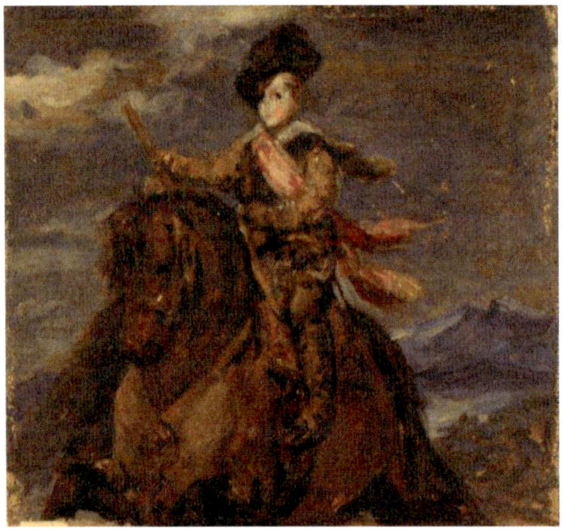

Fig. 14 Krehbiel's study of Velazquez work *Prince Baltasar Carlos on Horseback,* 1906, 7 ½ x 8, oil on board.

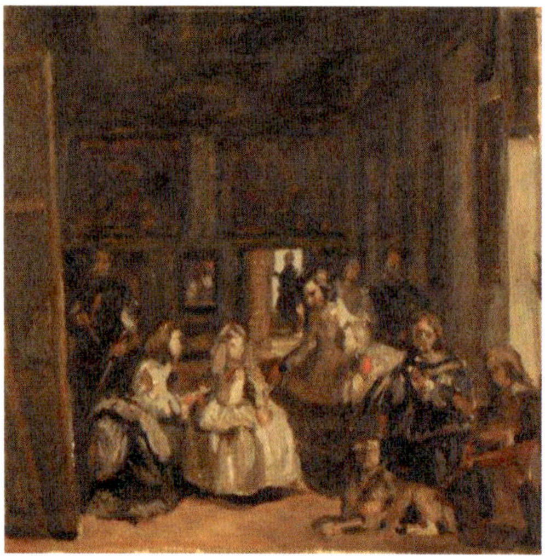

Fig. 15 Krehbiel's study of Velazquez work *Las Meninas,* 1906, 8 x 8, oil on board.

Krehbiel Returns Home – His Mural Works

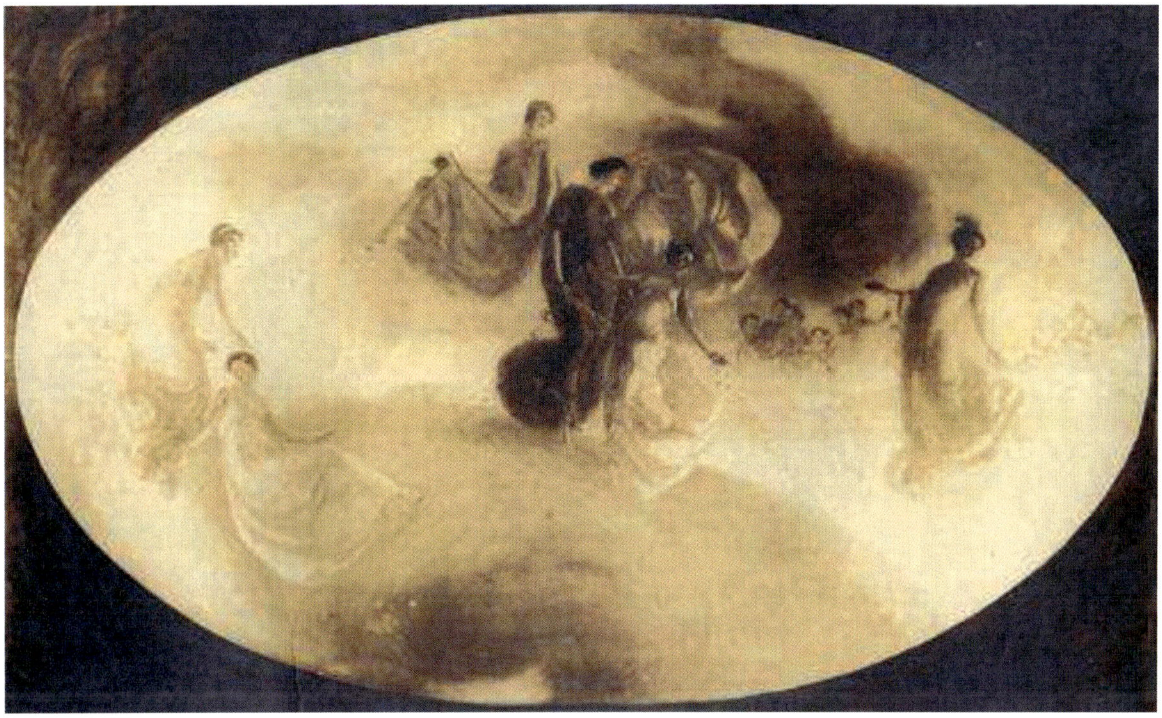

Fig. 16 Albert Krehbiel's first mural (from black and white archive photo) created for the dining room ceiling of the family residence of Hugo Leisy, Cleveland, Ohio, 1906, oil on canvas.

Returning to the United States in May of 1906, Krehbiel rejoined the faculty of The Art Institute of Chicago at the urging of Mr. French. On June 5th, he married his beloved Dulah, a highly talented artist in her own right. After graduating from The Art Institute, Dulah was a resident of the Tree Studio Building in Chicago from 1903 through 1905. Continuing her education, she studied in New York at the Art Students League and at the New York School of Art under William Merritt Chase (1849-1916). Dulah went on to have an extremely accomplished career as a painter, printmaker, and commercial artist *(see Figs. 17, 18, and 19 and Figs. 40 and 41 on page 17)*.

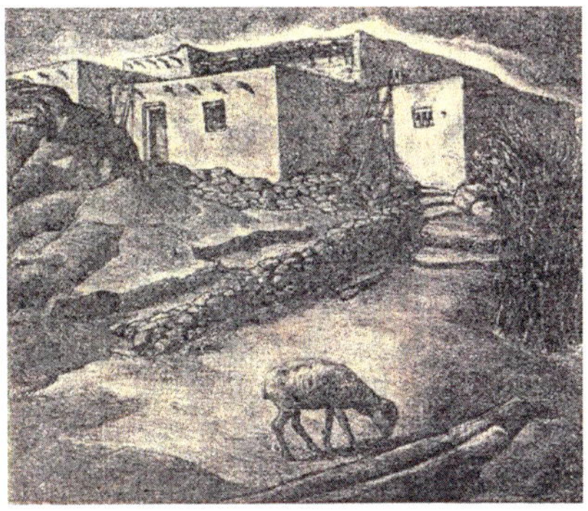

Fig. 17 *Indian Home, Laguna Pueblo* (from black and white archive photo), Dulah Marie Evans (Krehbiel), Laguna, New Mexico, 1927, 8½ x 10½, lithograph.

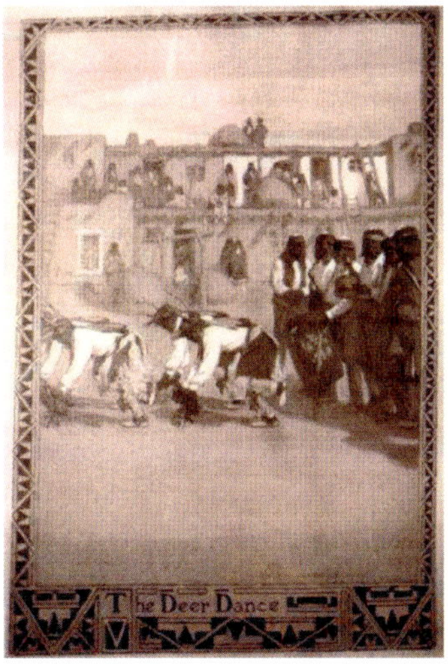

Fig. 18 *The Deer Dance* (from black and white archive photo), Dulah Marie Evans, Tesuque, New Mexico, ca. 1906, size not known, oil on canvas.

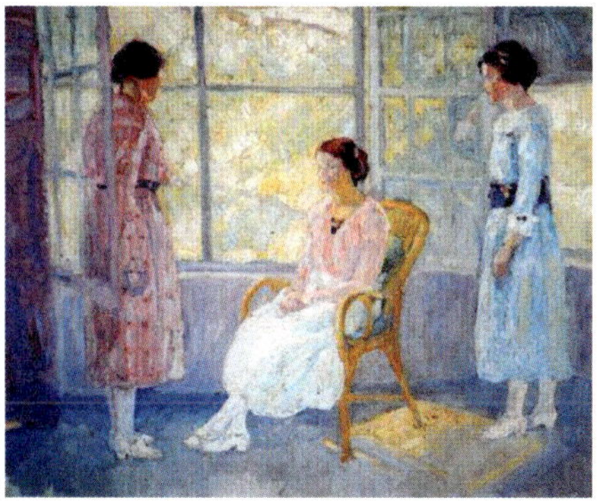

Fig. 19 *Three Ladies at an Open Window*, Dulah Marie Evans (Krehbiel), Park Ridge, Illinois, August 1920, 14 x 17, oil on canvas. Courtesy of The National Museum of Women in the Arts, Washington, D.C.

While maintaining a full-time teaching schedule at The Art Institute in 1906, Krehbiel received the commission to design and paint the mural for the wall of the Juvenile Court Room in Chicago *(see Fig. 20)*. The scene depicted in the Juvenile Court mural appears to express the carefree joy of youth in a lawful, independent, and free land. The farmer tending his field in the background seems to represent the opportunity for all to prosper in a nation founded on the principles of democracy and free enterprise, while the adults in the left background overseeing the children reflects the importance of family values and parental supervision.

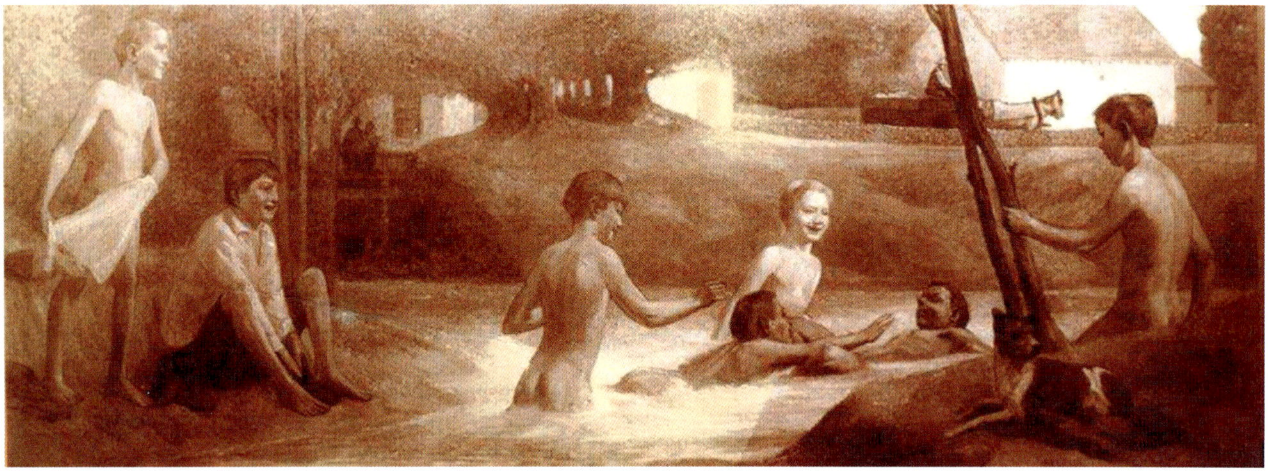

Fig. 20 Krehbiel's mural for the wall of the Chicago Juvenile Court Room (from black and white photo), Chicago, Illinois, 1906, oil on canvas.

In 1907, having completed the Juvenile Court mural in his spare time from instruction, Krehbiel entered works in the competition to design and paint the eleven wall and two ceiling murals for the Supreme and Appellate Court Rooms at the Illinois Supreme Court Building in Springfield, the state's capitol. A total of twenty-two designs were submitted from some of the best artists throughout the United States. Krehbiel's design proposal for the murals included six themes depicting the *Origin, Function, and Continuity of Law,* including: *Origins of Law*, *The Continuity of Law*, *Function of Law, Attributes of Law*, *The Return of the Golden Age*, and *Law and Equity*. The work was classically inspired and consisted of men and woman portrayed as allegorical figures. The Jury of Awards was unanimous in granting the commission to Albert H. Krehbiel.

Reducing his teaching schedule to summer sessions only, Krehbiel, with Dulah's help, spent four years on the research, preparation, and composition of the Illinois Supreme and Appellate Court murals, which evolve into designs quite different from what he had originally planned. Having purchased a home in Park Ridge (a town ten miles northwest of Chicago), they bought an adjacent vacant lot, had a barn moved onto the property, and converted it into a studio *(see Fig. 21 on page 10)*. Large canvases were ordered from Paris and pulleys and scaffolds were constructed for the hanging and rolling of the canvases *(see Fig. 22 on page 10)*. Dulah created Grecian gowns and robes, posing in them so that their draping would appear authentic *(see Fig. 23 on page 11)*.

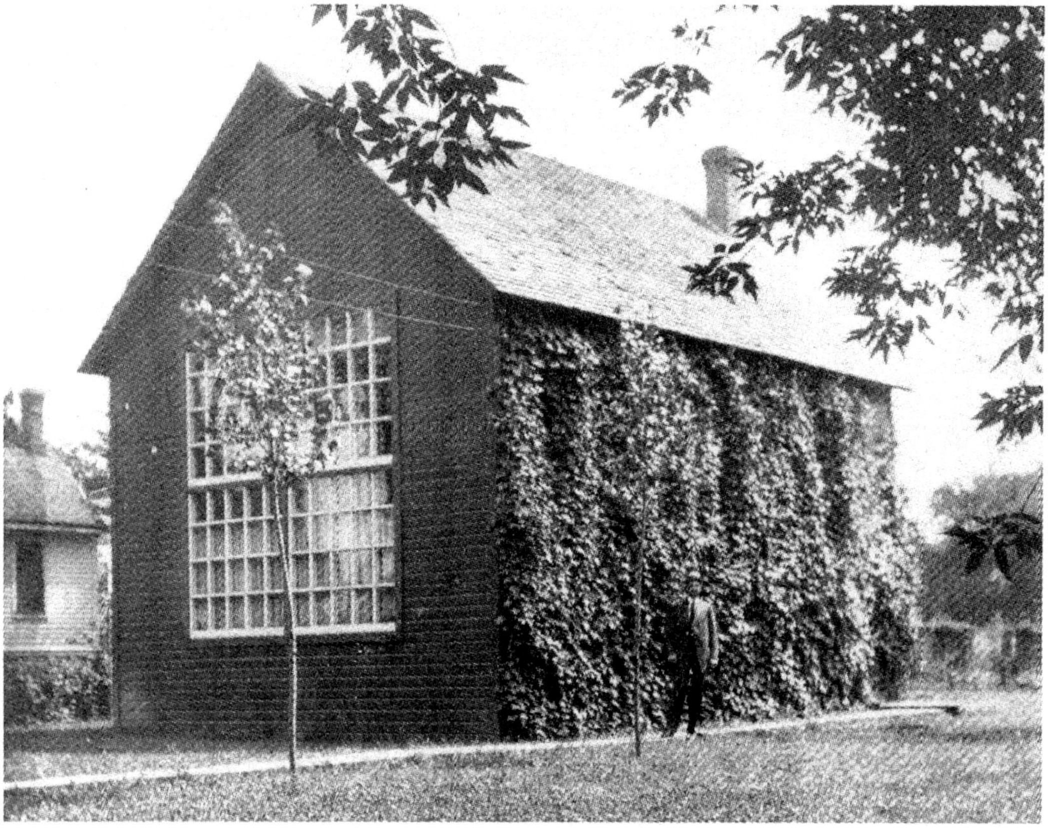

Fig. 21 Krehbiel standing beside his Park Ridge studio, where he designed and painted the mural panels for the Illinois Supreme Court Building.

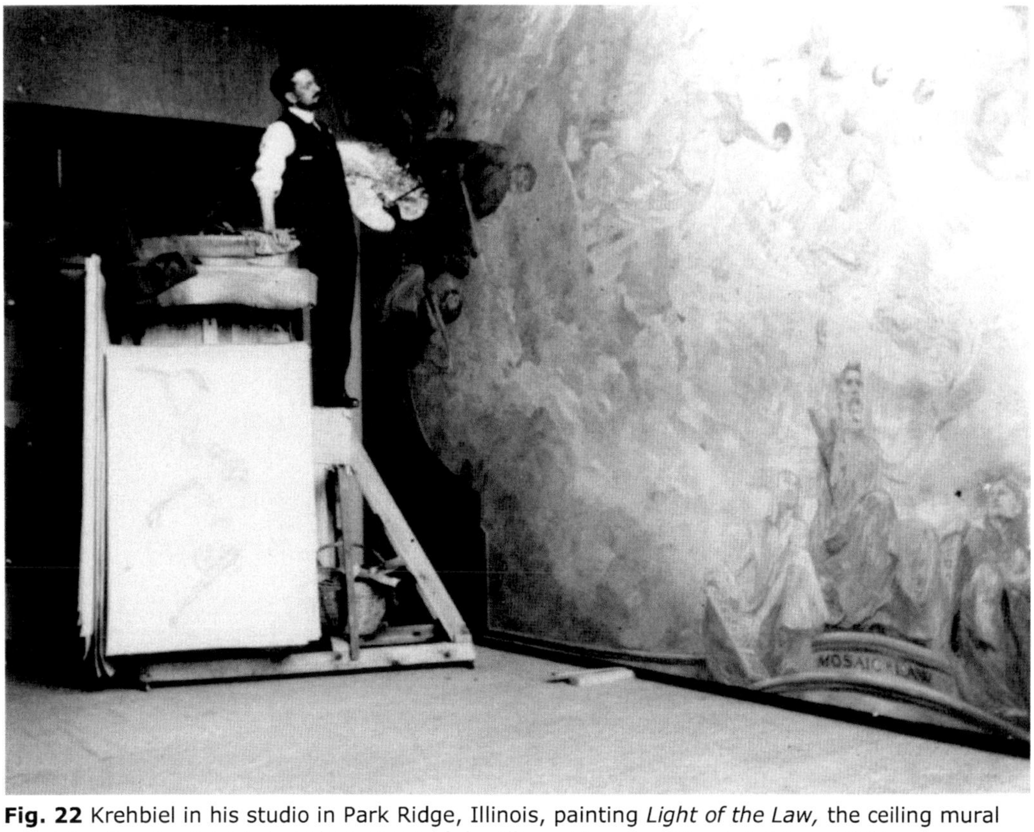

Fig. 22 Krehbiel in his studio in Park Ridge, Illinois, painting *Light of the Law,* the ceiling mural panel for Fourth District Appellate Court of the Illinois Supreme Court Building, 1910.

Upon the completion of each of the thirteen murals, the canvas was transported to Springfield and installed. The final mural was completed and installed in 1911. *(See Fig. 24 and Figs. 25 through 29 on pages 12 and 13.)*

Mr. W. Carby Zimmerman, architect of the Supreme Court Building, considered the work done by Krehbiel to be "an example of the best mural painting ever executed in the West". In ***Art Across America, Two Centuries of Regional Painting, 1710-1920***, (Volume Two; Abbeville Press, New York; p. 319), author William Gerdts states:

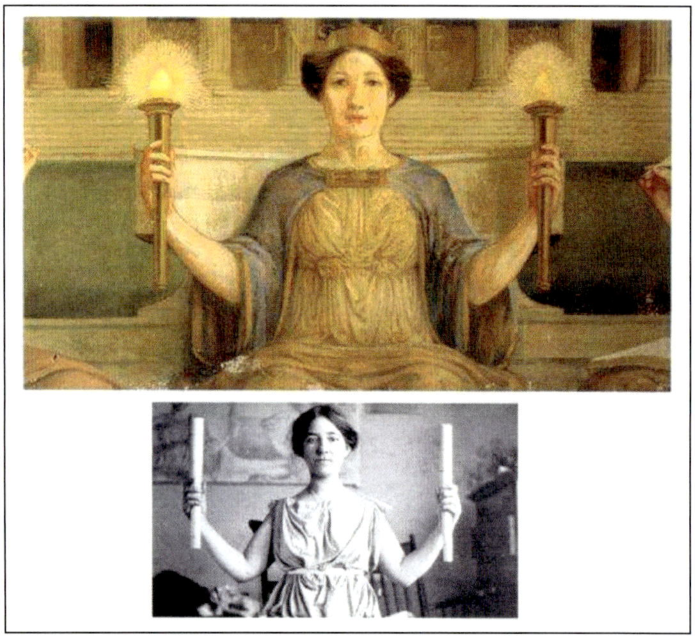

Fig. 23 Dulah Evans Krehbiel posing as an allegorical figure for a study for Albert Krehbiel's Illinois Supreme Court wall mural *Justice With Precedence and Record*, (detail), Park Ridge, Illinois, ca. 1909.

***". . . (Frederic Clay)* Bartlett may share the distinction as Chicago's most renowned muralist of the early twentieth century with Albert Krehbiel."**

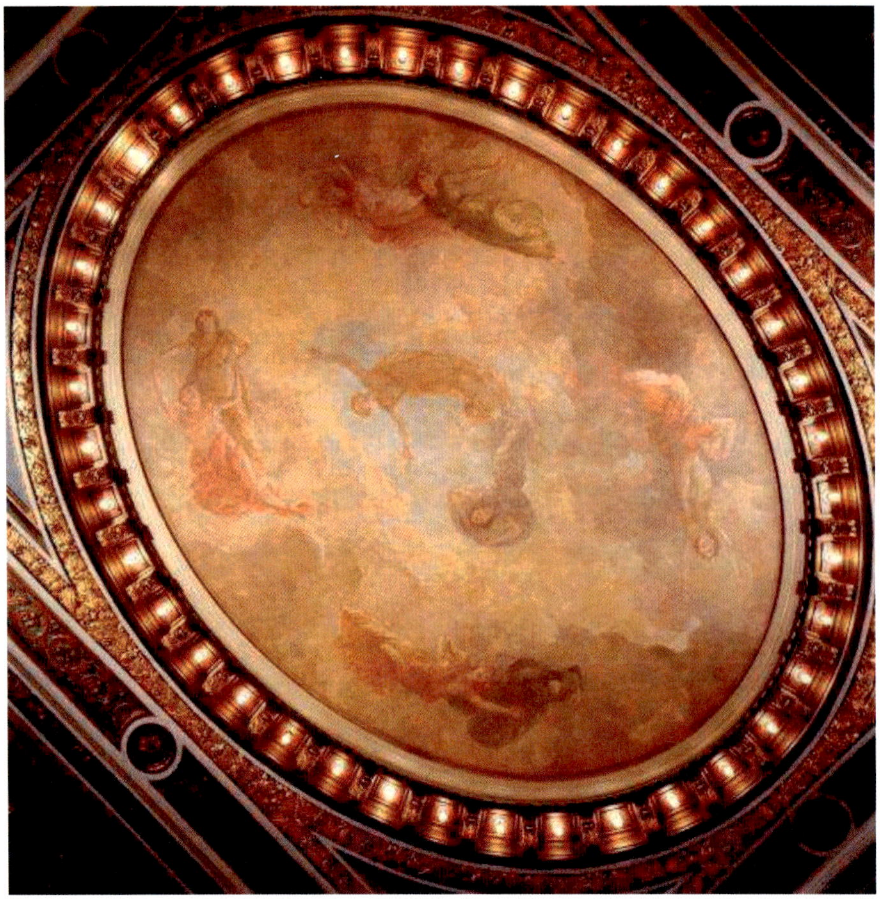

Fig. 24 *Supremacy of the Law,* ceiling mural in the Illinois Supreme Court, Springfield, Illinois, 1907-1911, 21 ft. x 16 ft., oil on canvas.

"The mural symbolizes the principles of law that serve to harmonize the universe. *Good and Evil* are in the center, surrounded by storm clouds with light and dark depicting the changing phases of nature. *Good* soars free and victorious; *Evil* looms veiled and defeated. A cycle of four laws revolves around the pair. *Law of Love* appears as a mother ministering maternal love to her child. *Law of Self-Preservation* is depicted by a chief figure warding off impending danger. *Law of Life and Death* details *Death* pursuing *Life*, who soars unaware of *Death's* swift approach. The fourth group, *Law of Evolution*, is represented by two figures rising out of darkness toward light." 3

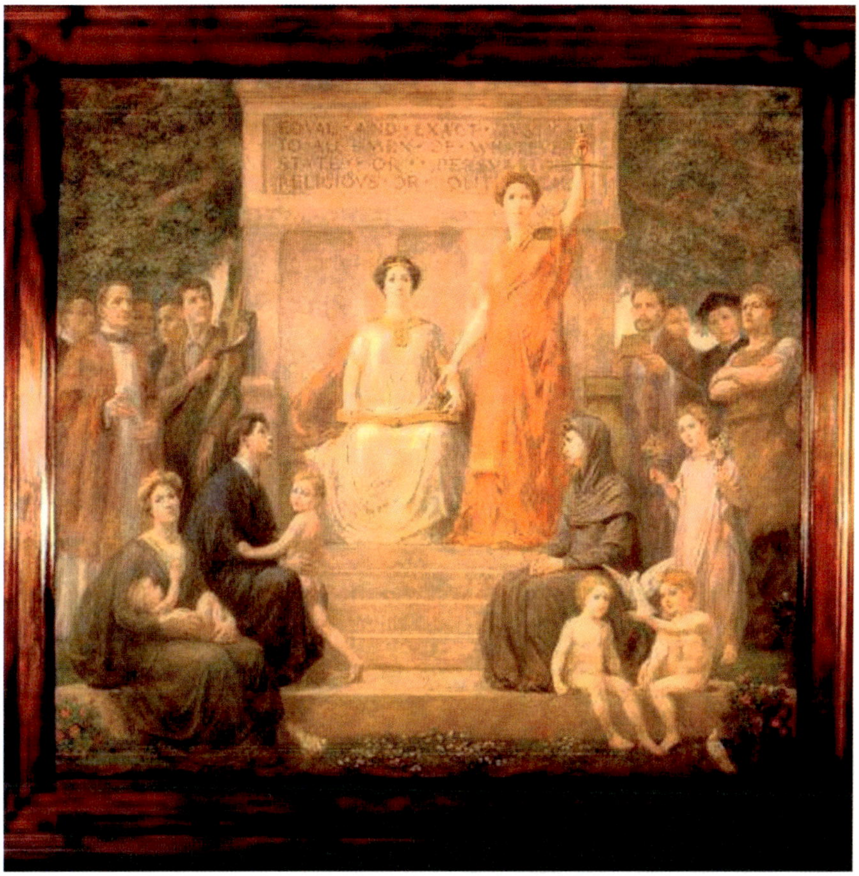

Fig. 25 *Law and Equity*, wall mural in the Fourth District Appellate Court of the Illinois Supreme Court Building, Springfield, Illinois, 1907-1911, 10 ft. x 16 ft., oil on canvas.

"Allegorical figures *Law* and *Justice* are enthroned on a stone dais. *Justice* holds her scales high while pointing to the printed statutes held by *Law*." 3 Inscribed over the central figures of the mural is a quote from Thomas Jefferson that reads:

"Equal and exact justice to all men of whatever state or persuasion, religious or political." 3

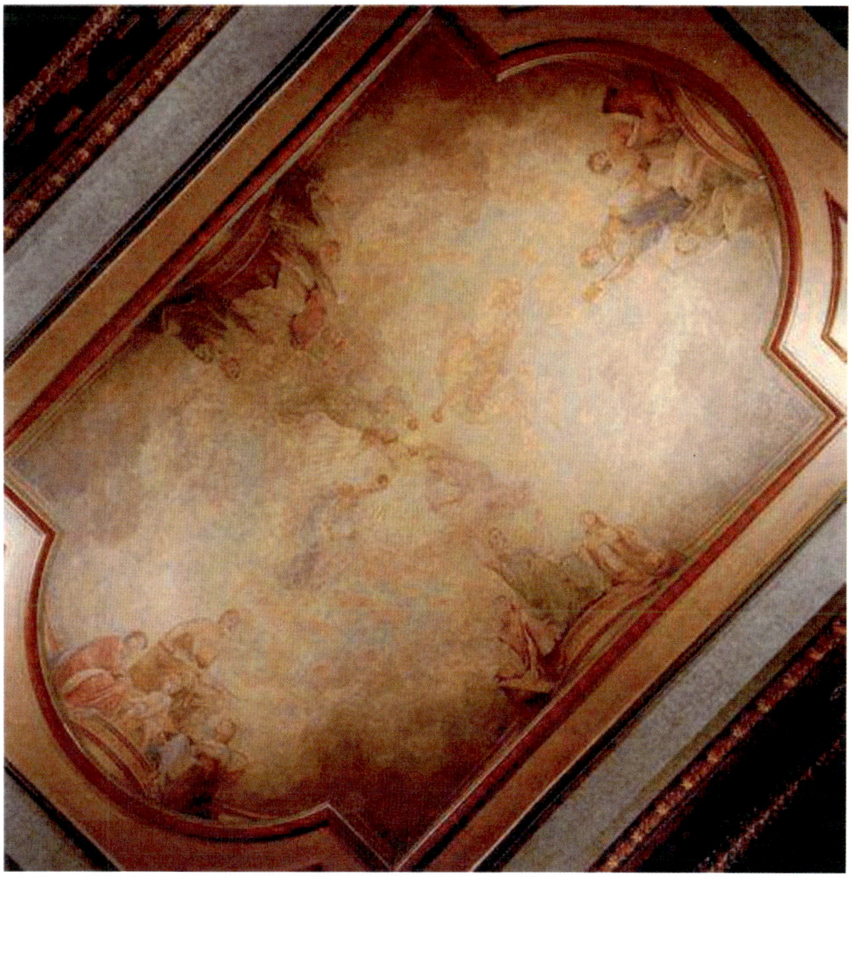

Fig. 26 *Light of the Law,* ceiling mural in The Fourth District Appellate Court of the Illinois Supreme Court Building, Springfield, Illinois, 1907-1911, 16 ft. x 26 ft., oil on canvas.

"From the center radiates the *Light of the Law*, around which cluster graceful figures offering torches to the four groups of figures arranged along the border, each symbolizing a tenet of American jurisprudence: *Common Law and the Light of Reason*, represented by Alfred the Great; *Canon Law and the Light of Inspiration*, represented by Pope Gregory IX*; Civil Law and the Light of Order*, represented by Justinian I; and *Mosaic Law*, represented by Moses." 3

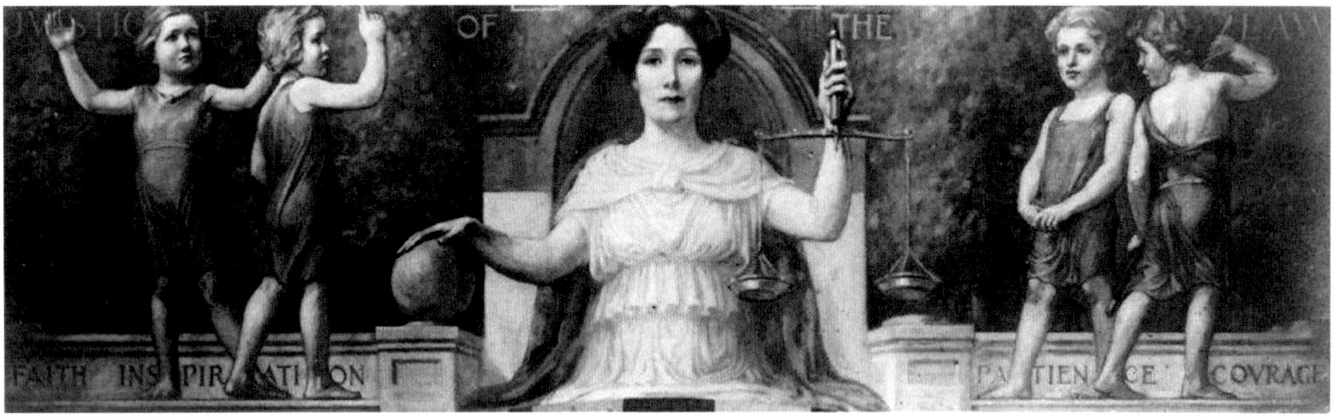

Fig. 27 *Justice of the Law – Faith and Inspiration, Patience and Courage* (from black and white photo), one of the three murals displayed on the east wall of the Illinois Supreme Court depicting the "Attributes of Law", Springfield, Illinois, 1907-1911, oil on canvas. "Each theme is represented by a seated woman with other qualities expressed by the classical figures known as *genni."* 3

Figs. 28 and 29 Two of the four panels on the south wall of the Illinois Supreme Court titled *Function of the Law.* "The backgrounds of these murals are extremely expressive – the first two show peaceful scenes of trees and grass *(see Fig. 28)*; the other two show backgrounds that are rugged and threatening *(see Fig. 29)."* 3

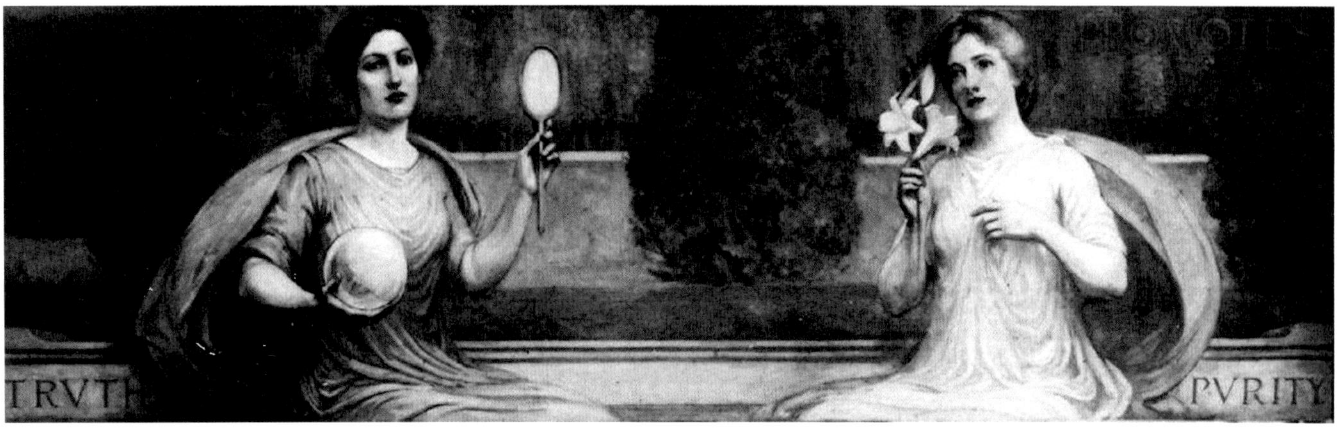

Fig. 28 *Law Promotes – Truth and Purity* (from black and white photo), wall mural in the Illinois Supreme Court, Springfield, Illinois, 1907-1911, oil on canvas.

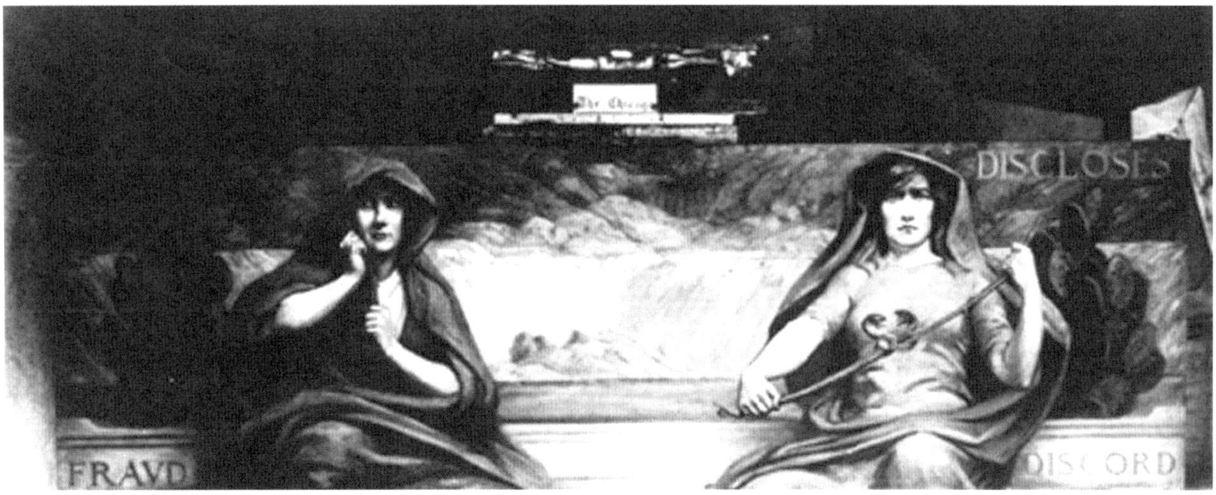

Fig. 29 *Law Discloses – Fraud and Discord* (from black and white photo), wall mural in the Illinois Supreme Court, Springfield, Illinois, 1907-1911, oil on canvas.

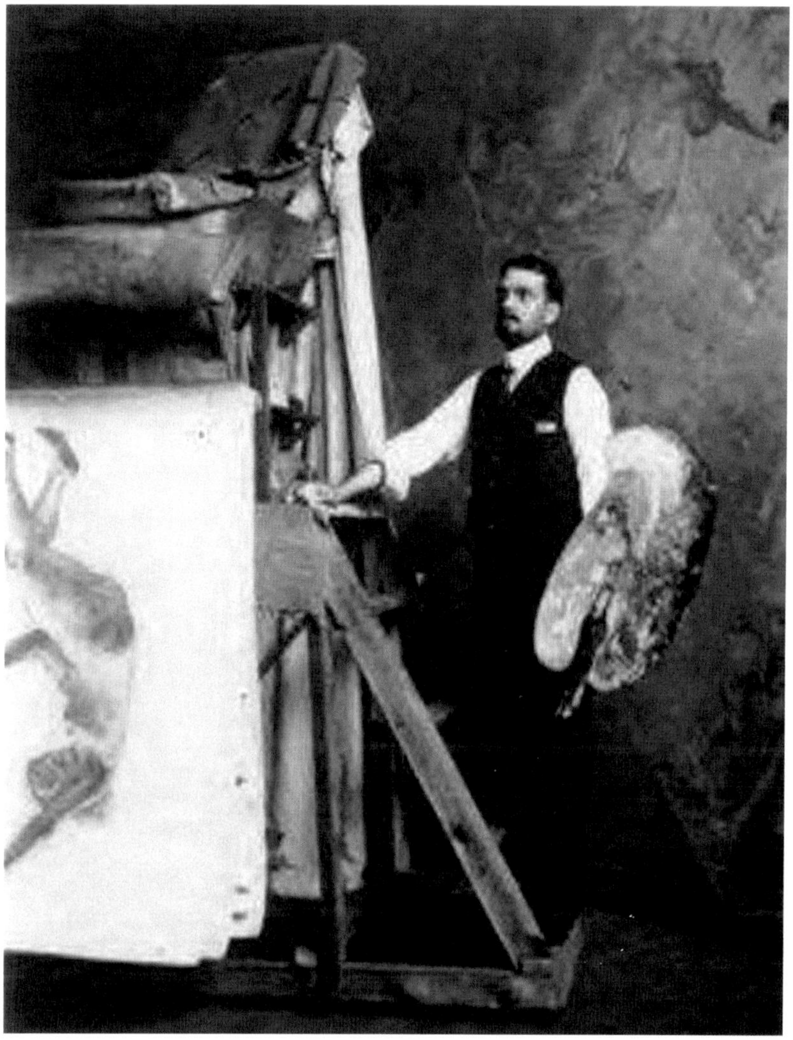

Fig. 30 Krehbiel in his Park Ridge studio at work on *Light of the Law,* the ceiling mural panel for the Fourth District Appellate Court Room at the Illinois Supreme Court Building (*see Fig. 26, page 12*).

Krehbiel returned to full time instruction at the Art Institute in 1911, teaching students about the use of color, design, and space. In 1913, he also joined the faculty of the Armour Institute of Technology (later named the Illinois Institute of Technology) as an instructor of architectural drawing. It is here that Krehbiel, many years later in 1938, developed a close friendship with architect Ludwig Mies van der Rohe. Having left Germany in 1937 for the United States, Mies van der Rohe headed the department of architecture at the Armour Institute from 1938 until his retirement in 1958. Krehbiel, notably, was the only in-place instructor that Mies van der Rohe kept on the staff. Speaking in German, at which Krehbiel was fluent, they would frequently discuss their work over martinis at the Cliff Dwellers, an important Chicago artistic social club of which they were both members (and where Krehbiel then resides), with Mies van der Rohe puffing away at a cigar and Krehbiel smoking his pipe.

Impressionistic Transition - Painting Outdoors in Park Ridge, Santa Monica, and Santa Fe

"Shortly after completing the Illinois Supreme Court Murals, Krehbiel's work changed direction. Instead of painting entirely in his studio, he began to seek the outdoors and to paint the atmospheric effects of sun, fog, and snow, with broad visible brush strokes. It was at this time that Krehbiel began to incorporate the principles of impressionism into his work." 1 A few examples of his transitional works are *Two Ladies in the Grape Arbor (Fig. 31), Lady and Her Bowl of Nasturtiums (Fig. 32),* and *Away to Fairyland (Fig. 33)*. "Here, Krehbiel painted casual color scenes with a naturalistic approach that, at the same time, had sharp contours and shading of drapery folds recalling the principles of a more classical 19th century academic manner of presentation. However, the heightened color tone levels along with the subdued quality of the trees and landscape suggest that he was experimenting with some of the techniques established by the impressionists of France and their followers in America." 1

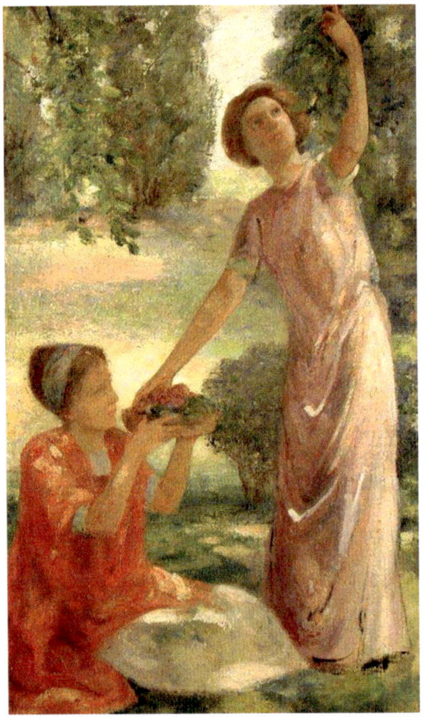

Fig. 31 *Two Ladies in the Grape Arbor*, Park Ridge, Illinois, ca. 1913, 32 x 19, oil on canvas.

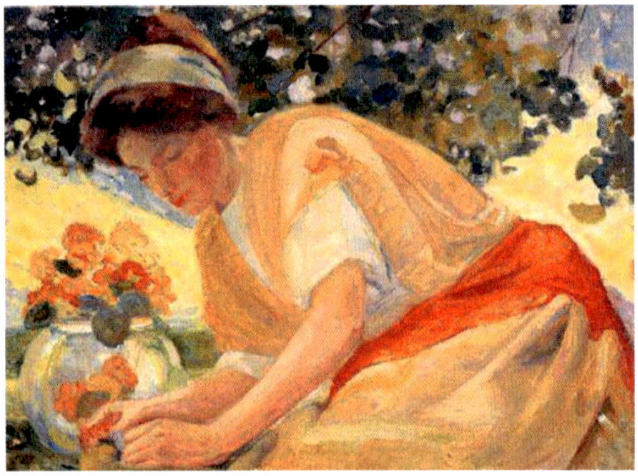

Fig. 32 *Lady and Her Bowl of Nasturtiums*, Park Ridge, Illinois, ca. 1914, 22 x 30, oil on canvas.

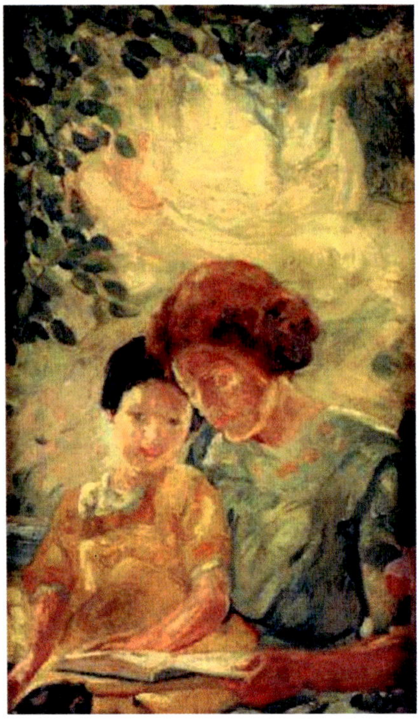

Fig. 33 *Away to Fairyland,* Park Ridge, Illinois, ca. 1913, 33 x 20, oil on canvas.

Beginning in 1918 and continuing through the early 1920s, Krehbiel spent a good part of his summers at an art colony in Santa Monica, California, with Dulah, Evans (their son and only child), and Dulah's sister, Mayetta, where he painted impressionistic high-keyed shoreline views and landscapes *(see **California Works,** Figs. 34 through 39)* while Dulah painted her son and sister in various settings *(see Figs. 40 and 41 on page 17)*. "The continuing shift in Krehbiel's approach becomes more pronounced in his California works. The light-flooded scenes conveyed by thick impasto brushwork emphasize the play of juxtaposed contrasting colors. There is a reduced concentration on the modeling of three-dimensional shapes, and the boundaries between individual objects soften." 1

California Works
Figs. 34 through 39

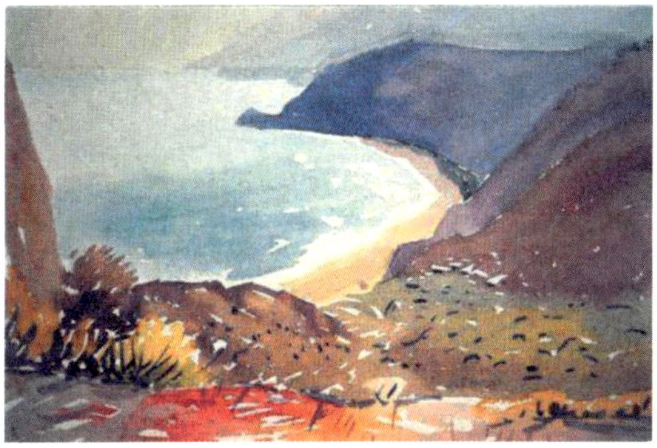

Fig. 34 *Purple Mountain Mystery,* ca. 1918, 10 x 12, watercolor on paper.

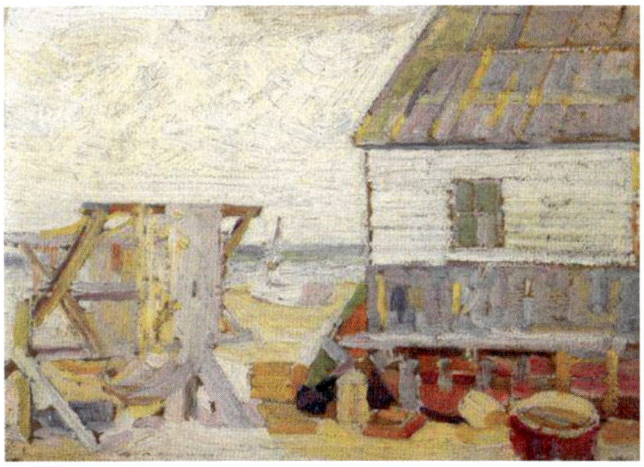

Fig. 35 *Drying Nets*, 1918, 9½ x 12½, oil on board.

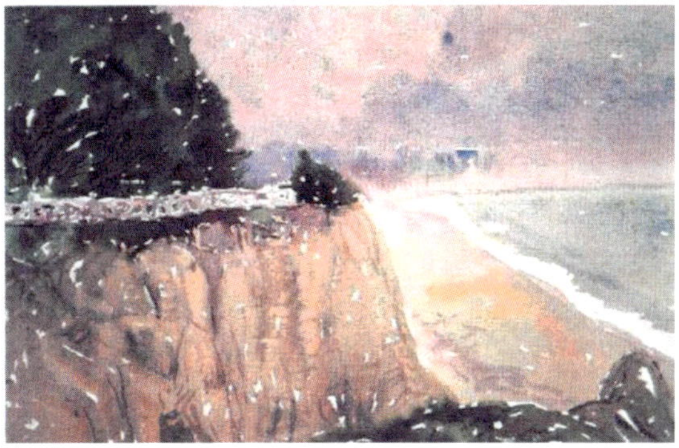

Fig. 36 *Looking Across Park Balustrade,* ca. 1918, 9 x 12, watercolor on paper.

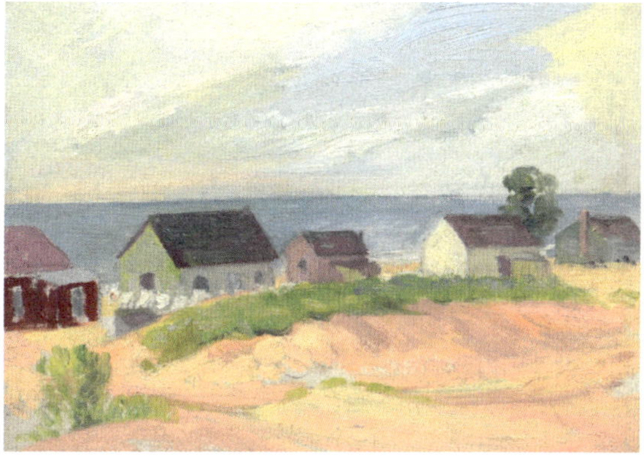

Fig. 37 *Untitled (Beach Cottages)*, ca. 1918, 9½ x 12½, oil on board.

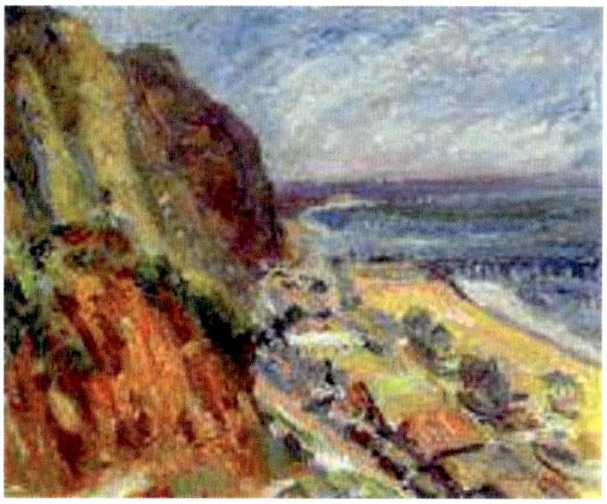

Fig. 38 *California Village Along Coast,* 1922, 14 x 17, oil on canvas.

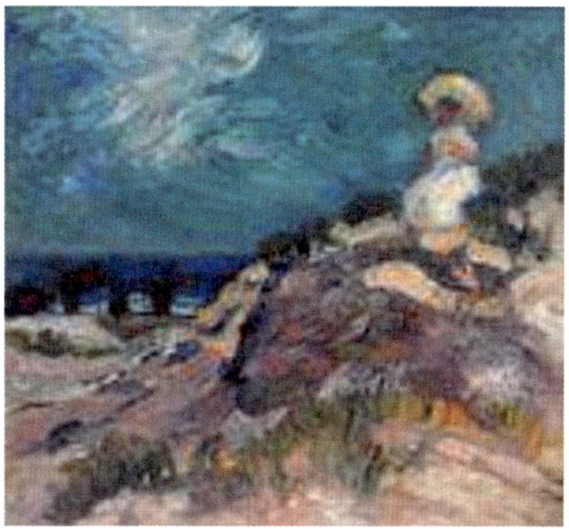

Fig. 39 *Seashore Romance,* ca. 1918, 8½ x 8½, oil on board.

Krehbiel spent the balance of the summers of 1918 through 1921 in Santa Fe, New Mexico. From 1920 through 1923 - at times again traveling with Dulah, Evans, and Mayetta - Krehbiel was an exhibiting member of the Santa Fe Art Colony. "He was very well respected as an artist in Santa Fe, as well as in Chicago, during these years. In 1922 and 1923, Krehbiel was invited to Santa Fe by the Museum of New Mexico to participate in its Visiting Artists Program and given a studio in the historic Palace of the Governors next door to famed Ashcan realist, Robert Henri (1865-1929). In a letter from Santa Fe in 1922, Krehbiel wrote:

> ***'I must tell you of the many kindnesses I have received here from the friends of the museum . . . Dr. Hewett from the beginning has been gracious and allotted me one of the four studios maintained for visiting artists. Robert Henri, by the way, has been my neighbor.' "*** 4

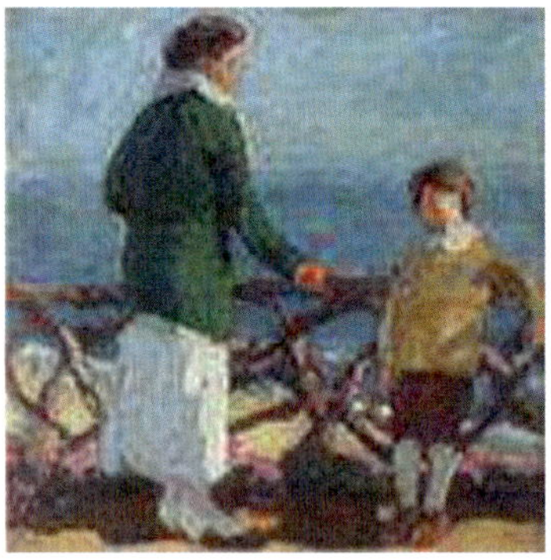

Fig. 40 *Evans and Mayetta Overlooking the Ocean*, Dulah Marie Evans (Krehbiel), Santa Monica, California, 1918, 8½ x 8½ , oil on canvas.

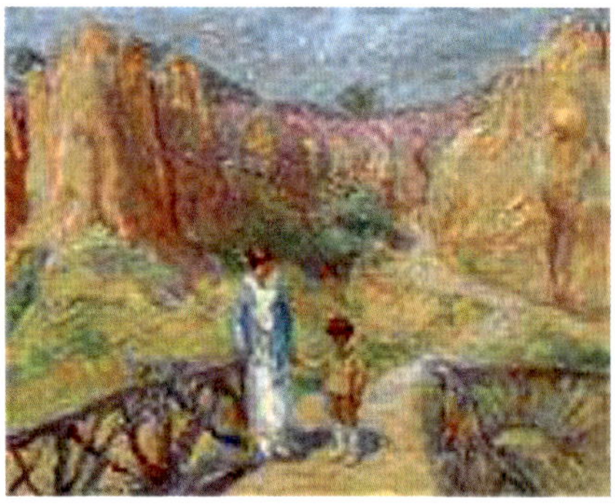

Fig. 41 *Santa Monica Bay*, Dulah Marie Evans (Krehbiel), Santa Monica, California, 1920, 18 x 21, oil on canvas.

"In his Santa Fe works, Krehbiel seemed to have delighted in the free use of color. Vibrant rhythmic brush strokes radiate from the canvas and color is used with the same strength in areas of light as it is in areas of shadow. The unnatural colors lend themselves to the dramatic sun-drenched landscapes of the Southwest." 1 *(See **Santa Fe Horseman**, Fig. 42, and **Santa Fe Works, Figs. 43 through 54**, on pages 18 and 19.)* In the same 1922 letter, Krehbiel continues:

> ***" . . . To me, the hours between daylight and sundown are for work – the charm of the light and color of this interesting country invite one to record its many-sided beauty without feeling fatigue."*** 4

Krehbiel had associations and exhibitions with other artists of the Santa Fe Art Colony -- and the Taos Society of Artists -- such as George Bellows and Gustave Baumann (exhibition in McPherson, Kansas, 1918), and B. J. O. Nordfeldt, Marsden Hartley, and Sheldon Parsons (exhibition in El Paso, Texas, 1920). Additional notable artists that Krehbiel exhibited with during this period include Victor Higgins, Earnest Blumenschein, John Sloan, Clarence Raymond Johnson, and Stuart Davis. 4

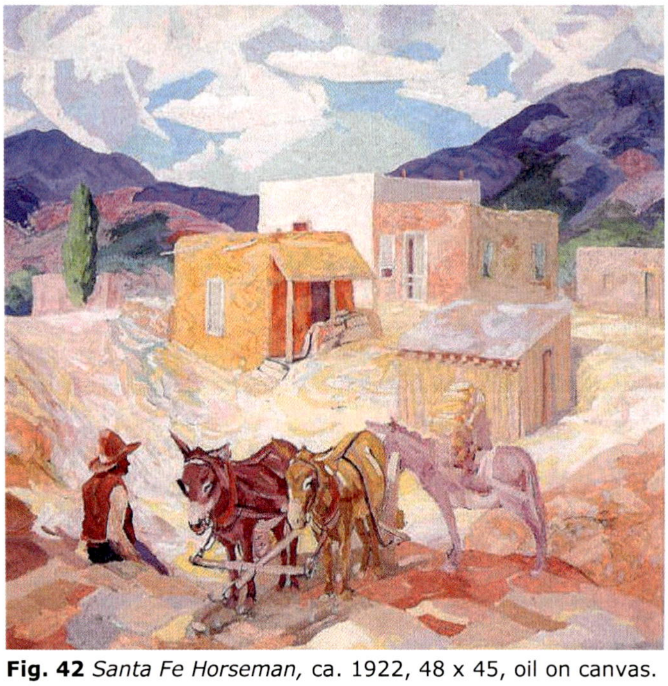

Fig. 42 *Santa Fe Horseman,* ca. 1922, 48 x 45, oil on canvas. Private collection.

Santa Fe Works Figs. 43 through 54

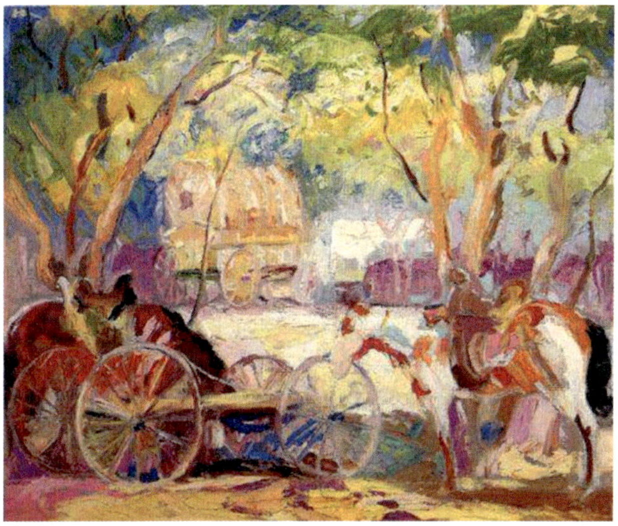

Fig. 43 *Circling the Wagons,* ca. 1922, 18 x 21, oil on canvas.

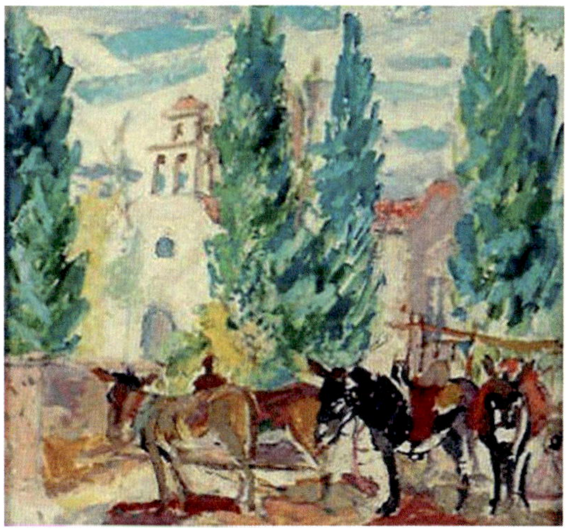

Fig. 44 *Waiting at the Church,* ca. 1922, 12 x 13, tempera on board.

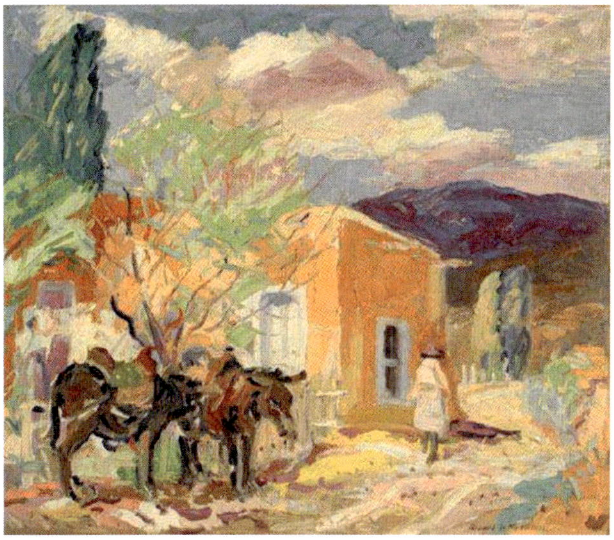

Fig. 45 *Tethered Mules,* ca. 1922, 18 x 21, oil on canvas.

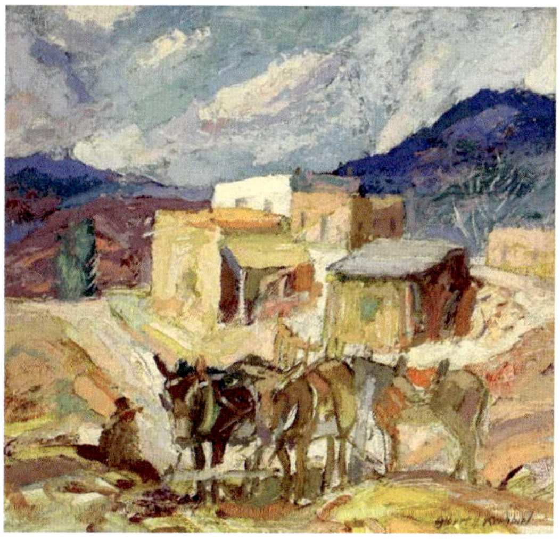

Fig. 46 *Study for Santa Fe Horseman,* ca. 1922, 12 x 13, tempera on board.

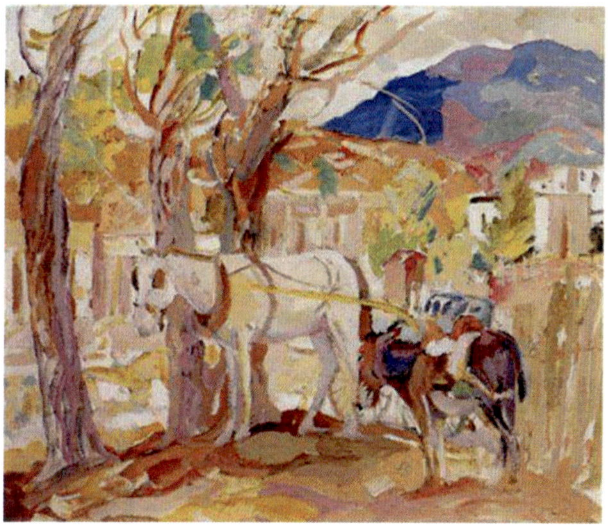

Fig. 47 *Forever Waiting,* ca. 1922, 18 x 21, tempera on canvas.

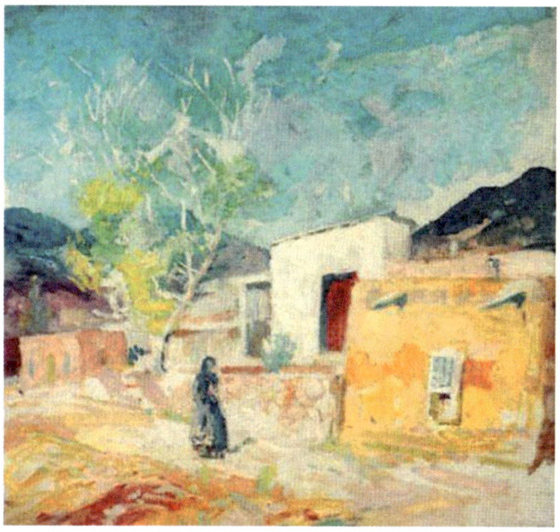

Fig. 48 *Santa Fe,* ca. 1922, 12 x 13, oil on board.

Santa Fe Works (continued)

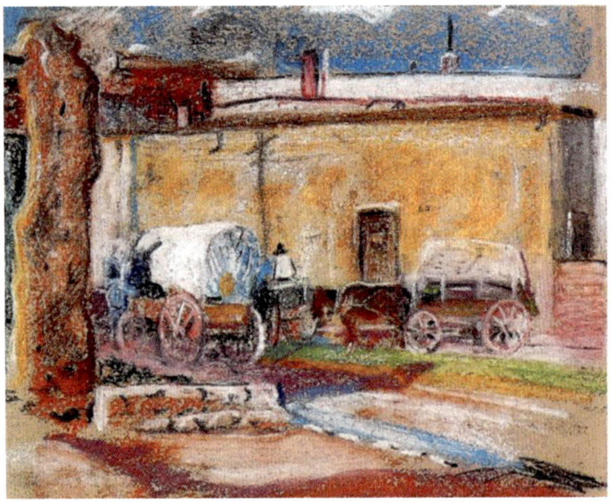

Fig. 49 *Heading for the Marketplace,* ca. 1922, 9 x 12, pastel on paper.

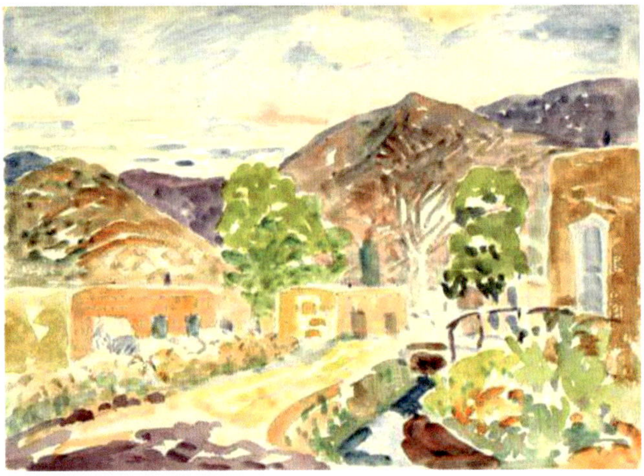

Fig. 50 *Pueblo Fantasy,* ca. 1923, 11 x 14, watercolor on paper.

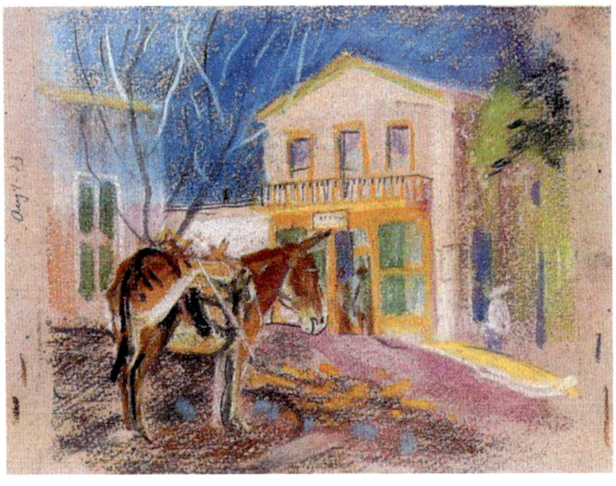

Fig. 51 *Pink Adobe with Mule in Front,* August 1, 1923, 9 x 12, pastel on paper.

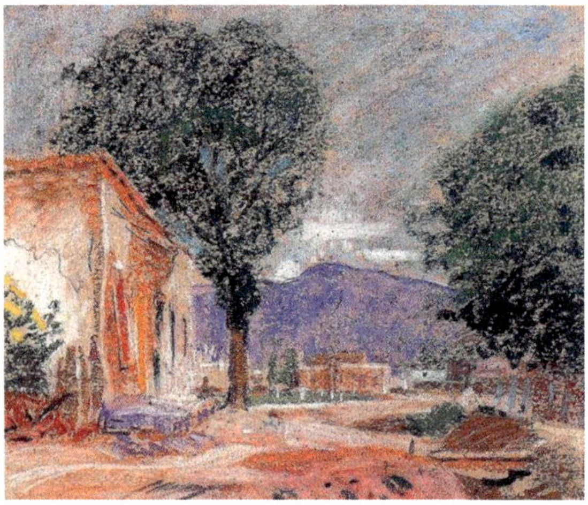

Fig. 52 *Village – Summer View,* ca. 1922, 9 x 12, pastel on paper.

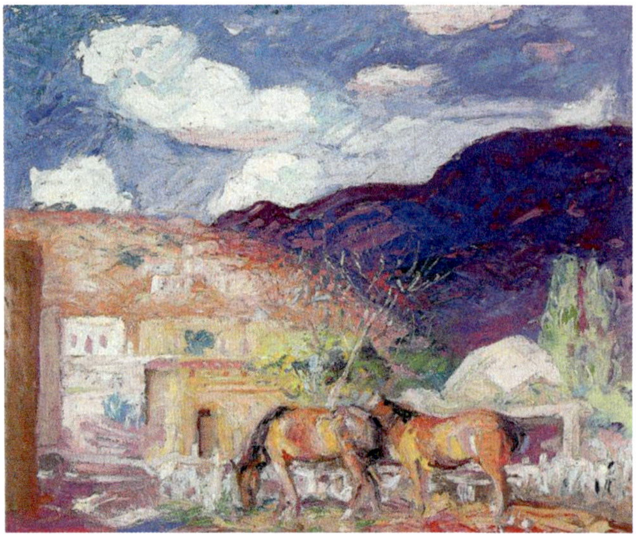

Fig. 53 *Purple Mountains – Animals Grazing,* ca. 1923, 18 x 21, oil on canvas.

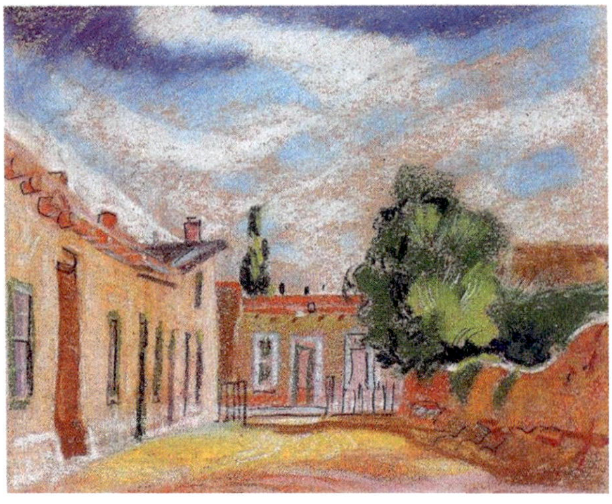

Fig. 54 *Hotel Eldorado,* August 22, 1923, 9 x 12 , pastel on paper.

Saugatuck, Michigan – Rolling Hills and the Kalamazoo River

In 1926, Krehbiel helped pioneer The Chicago Art Institute Summer School of Painting (later named Ox-Bow) in Saugatuck, Michigan. The school was founded as the Saugatuck School of Summer Painting in 1910 by a group of Chicago artists led by his friends and fellow instructors at The Art Institute of Chicago, Frederick Fursman (1874-1943) and Walter Marshall Clute (1870-1915). The summer migration of artists to Saugatuck began in 1900 when the daughter of the owner of one of the resort hotels invited some of her classmates from The Art Institute to vacation there. Among them were Albert Krehbiel and Dulah Evans. 2

"By the mid-1920s, the Saugatuck School had become the summer art mecca for commercial artists and architects from cities throughout the Midwest, as well as for students and alumni of The Art Institute." 2 Beginning in 1924, Saugatuck became an ever-increasing weekend and holiday retreat for Krehbiel and he spent most of his remaining summers teaching and painting there. In 1934, he opened his own summer school of art in Saugatuck called the AK Studio *(see Figs. 55 and 56)*.

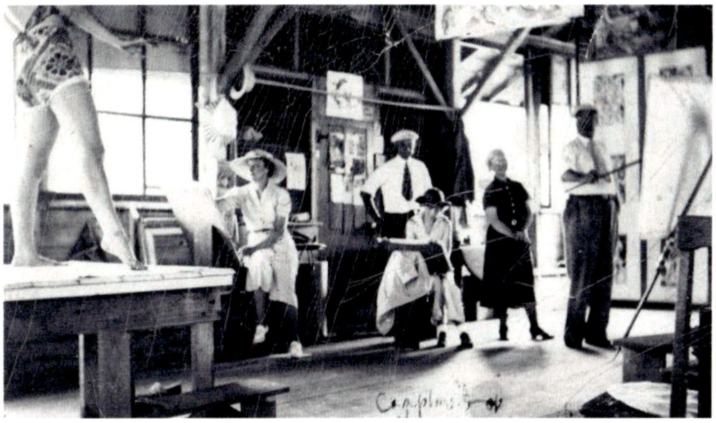

Fig. 55 Professor Krehbiel providing a drawing demonstration for a figure class at his AK Studio, Saugatuck, Michigan, 1938.

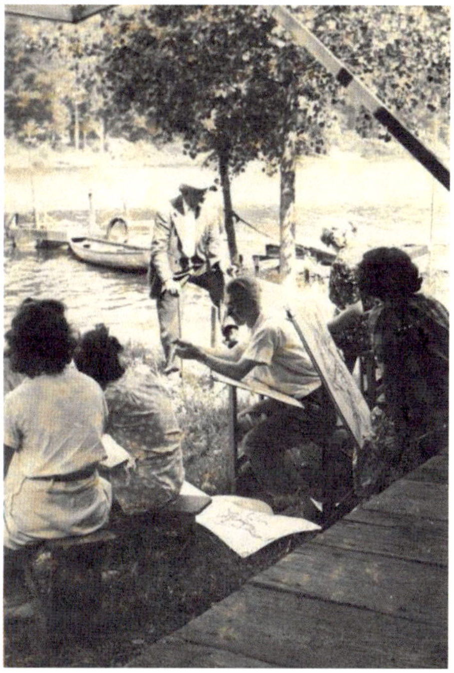

Fig. 56 Krehbiel conducting class in front of his studio along the banks of the Kalamazoo River, Saugatuck, Michigan, July 23, 1940.

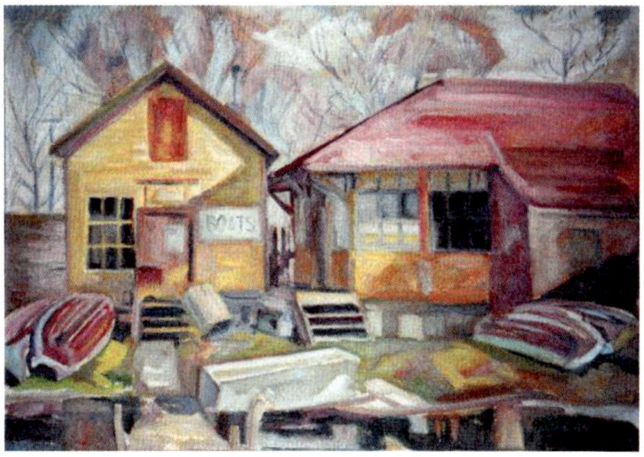

Right *Boat Houses*, Saugatuck, Michigan, 1938, 10 x 12, oil on canvas.

When able to free himself from his students in Saugatuck, Krehbiel painted many scenes overlooking the Kalamazoo River and the neighboring rolling hills as well as scenes with the hotels, shops, and homes lining the area's roads. These works capture the essence of the resort town with boats resting on the river's shore and rustic homes lying in the wooded landscape. During his winter visits, Krehbiel would portray Saugatuck in its vast and billowing cover of snow. *(See **Saugatuck Works, Figs. 57 through 62**, on page 21.)*

Saugatuck Works Figs. 57 through 62

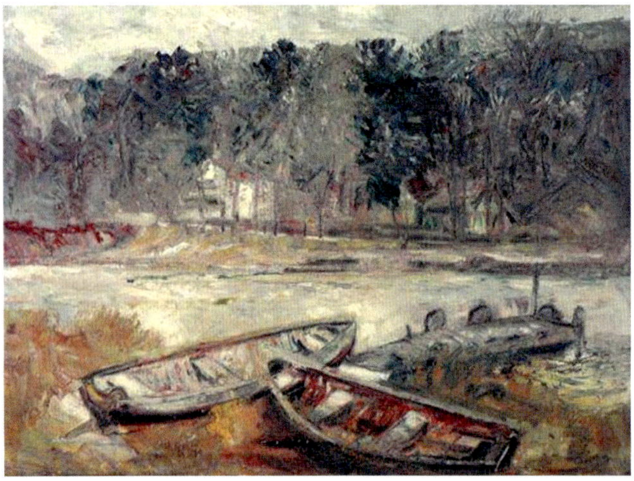

Fig. 57 *Row Boats Pulled Ashore,* 1941, 22 x 30, oil on canvas.

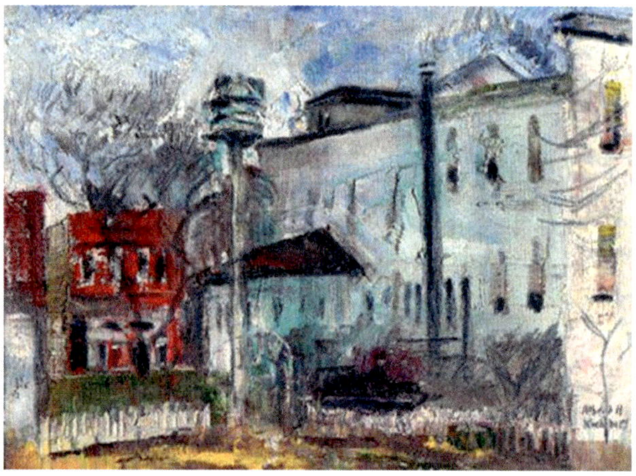

Fig. 60 *Resort Hotel Including a Martin House*, 1939, 9 x 12, oil on canvas.

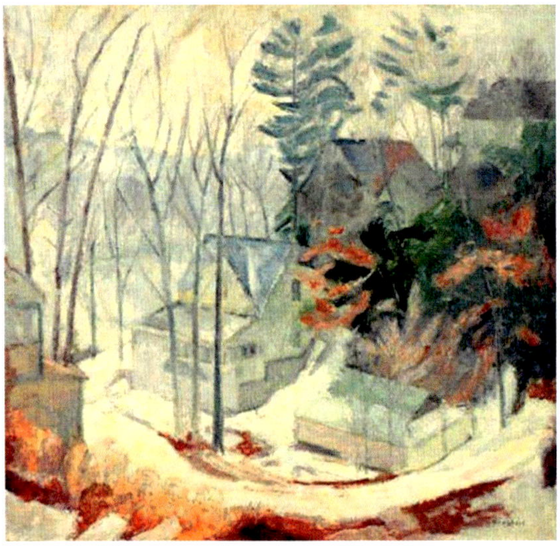

Fig. 58 *Summer Retreat in Winter,* 1936, 23 x 24, oil on canvas.

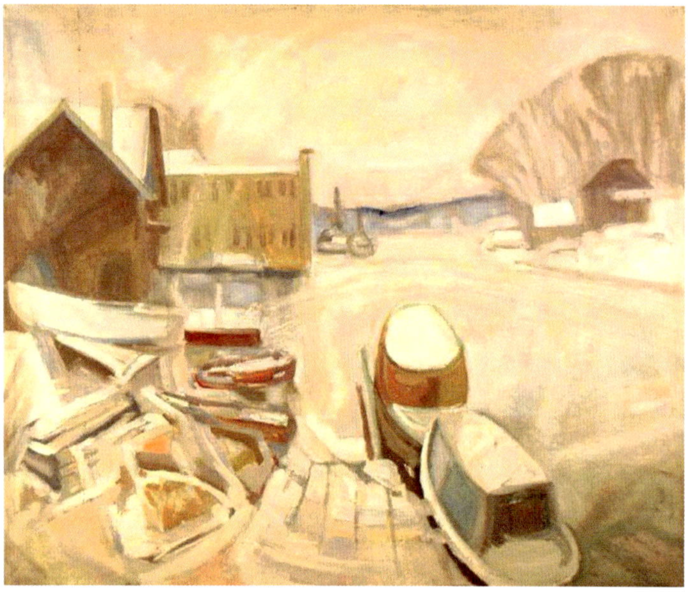

Fig. 61 *Beached for Winter's Ice,* ca. 1935, 36 x44, oil on canvas.

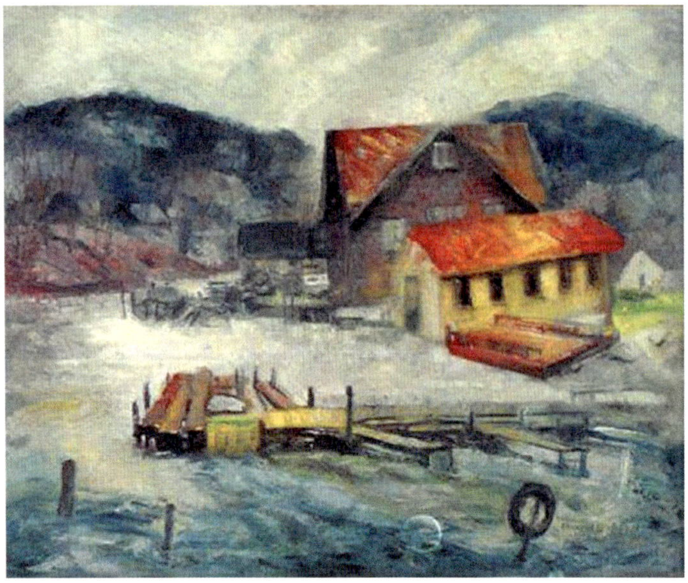

Fig. 59 *Summer Vacation,* 1939, 36 x 44, oil on canvas.

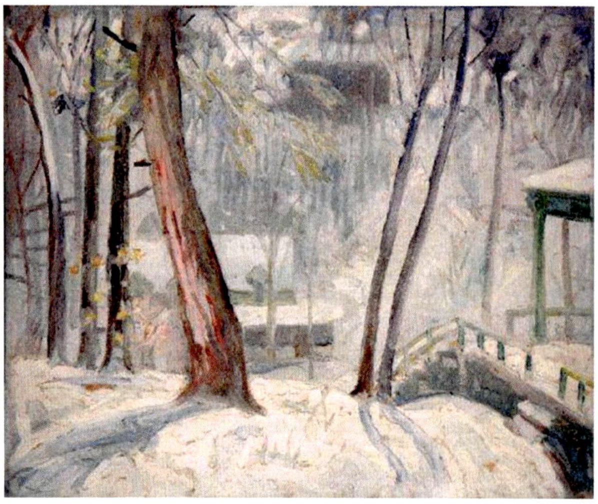

Fig. 62 *Homes on Rolling Hills in Winter,* 1930, 14 x 17, oil on canvas.

Throughout the 1980s, Marshall Salzman - a student of Krehbiel's at the AK Studio as well as at the Armour Institute in the late 1930s – wrote many letters to Rebecca F. Krehbiel, Albert Krehbiel's daughter-in-law. These letters reveal much about Krehbiel's character and his resolute dedication to the teaching and practice of drawing and painting. In one letter (not dated), Mr. Salzman writes:

> ***". . . Prof. K. gave a two-hour lecture to all graduating architects*** *(at the Illinois Institute of Technology)* ***at their request. Needless to say, he was happy to do this absolutely free. ...... Prof. K. and I were in the Saugatuck Studio on a Sunday*** *(when)* ***a chauffer-driven car pulled up in front and a well-groomed lady got out. ......She explained to Prof. K. that she represented a very fancy art group and was willing to pay him $300 to speak to her club for 30 minutes. In addition, her chauffer would pick him up and bring him back. Prof. K. said, 'if you would be kind enough to write your name and phone number on a piece of paper, I will call you within two days if I can make it. However, if I do not call, I will not be able to go.' She handed him the paper and thanked him. As the car drove off, he tore up the name and phone number and put it in the wastebasket. I asked what in the world he did that for since he gave our group a two-hour chalk talk every Saturday and we were paying so little. Prof. K. turned to me and said, 'I don't think they would understand what I was saying, and would make little use of what they might understand.' Wouldn't it be a great world if all teachers had that much integrity?"***

In another letter, Mr. Salzman writes of Krehbiel's entertaining ability at making drawing appear amazingly effortless and the reverence that his students felt for his talent:

> ***"......I remember one day we were all drawing nude compositions of a model. Prof. K. walked up to Miss Tibbs*** *(a student)* ***and said, ' You use this fine charcoal that is so thin it's almost like drawing with a pencil.' Then he said he was going to show her how to loosen up. This drew a crowd as we all gathered around, knowing a demonstration was in its way. He was fully aware of the total attention of the entire group. He said, 'I was going to tell you to use a larger charcoal, but I think it might be better for you to use your thumb', at which point he crushed a bunch of charcoal on the bench. Then he said, 'On second thought, I would like you to use the palm of your hand.' He rubbed his palm in the charcoal dust as he eyed the model and proceeded to put on a show that I had never seen before or since. In three strokes he drew the entire pose with the finest edge you've ever seen and shaded out to perfection. We all applauded and I think he was pleased with the result and our reaction to his skill."***

Fig. 63 Krehbiel observing his class at work in the AK Studio, Saugatuck, Michigan, 1940.

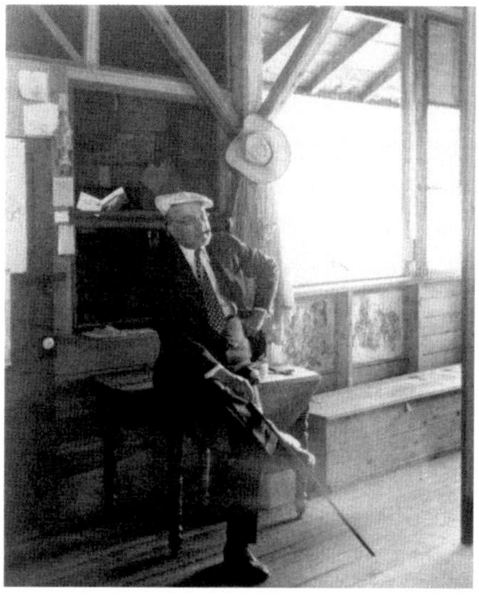

Illinois – Landscapes, Cityscapes, and Figures

Throughout the years when at home in Illinois, Krehbiel painted continuously. From his historic Chicago street and river scenes to his wooded presentations of the Midwest countryside and the hills and valleys of the northern Galena territory, he painted incessantly and in all seasons without regard for the elements.

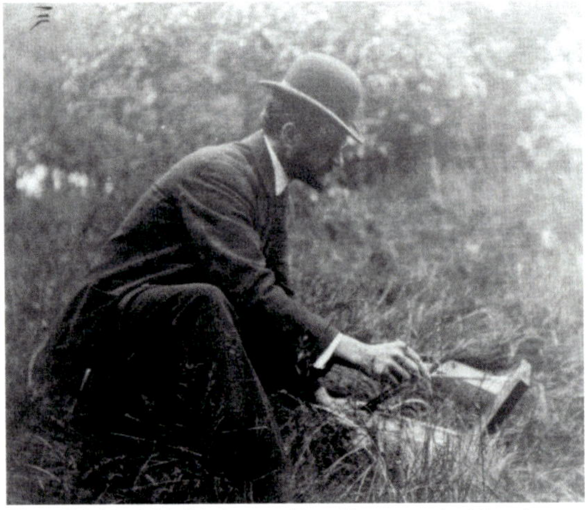

Fig. 64 Krehbiel interpreting the wooded landscape surrounding Park Ridge, Illinois, ca 1914.

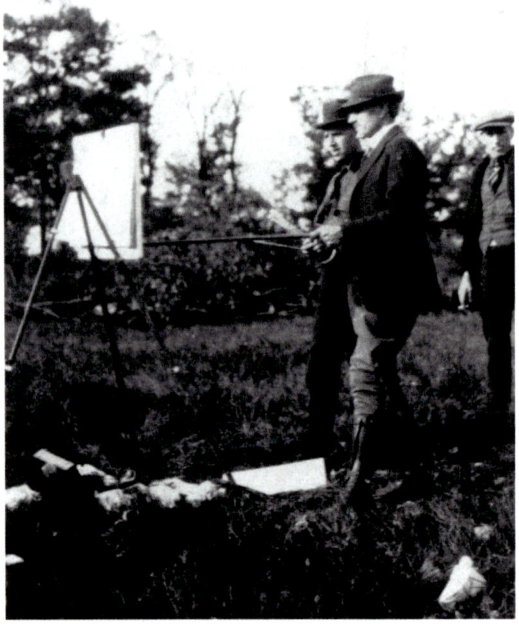

Fig. 65 Krehbiel instructing a class in a field in Edgebrook, a suburb just north of Chicago, 1924.

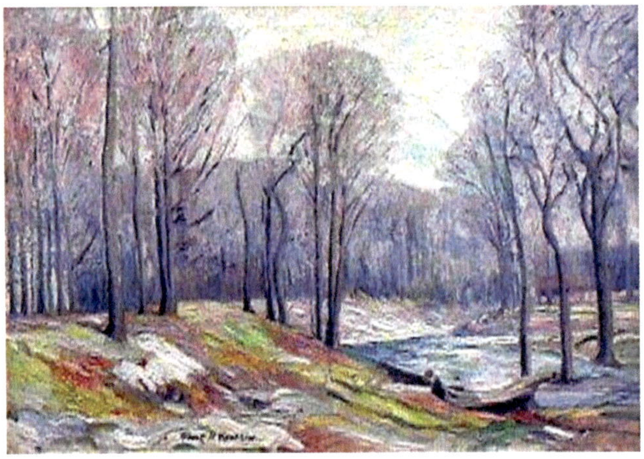

Left *Mild Winter on Des Plaines River,* Park Ridge, Illinois, ca. 1922, 22 x 30, oil on canvas. Courtesy of the John Vanderpoel Art Association, Chicago, Illinois.

"Like most American impressionists, Krehbiel did not subscribe to scientific color theories of the original French impressionists. Rather, he adopted other methods and lessons of impressionism. He was committed to painting outdoors in natural light and to capturing with a very personal vision the constantly changing character of the Midwest's landscape, done mainly in winter along the banks of the Chicago North Branch River and the Des Plaines River." [1] During the years of 1912 through about 1930, Krehbiel was known to leave his Park Ridge home on a freezing cold morning and not return until the end of the day with two or three freshly painted canvases of the surrounding landscape. *(See **Illinois Winter Scenes, Figs. 66 through 71**, on page 24.)* He also composed many oils, watercolors, and countless pastels of the area, often capturing the local inhabitants in the warmer months working in the fields or taking a moment to enjoy the lush forest landscape populated with brooks and streams *(see **Illinois Works, Figs. 72 through 83**, on pages 25 and 26)*. Occasionally, Krehbiel would visit the northern Illinois town of Galena on weekends and holidays to paint large canvases of the tree-covered hills with their scattering of homes and barns *(see **Galena Works, Figs. 84, 85, and 86**, on page 27)*.

Illinois Winter Scenes

Figs. 66 through 71

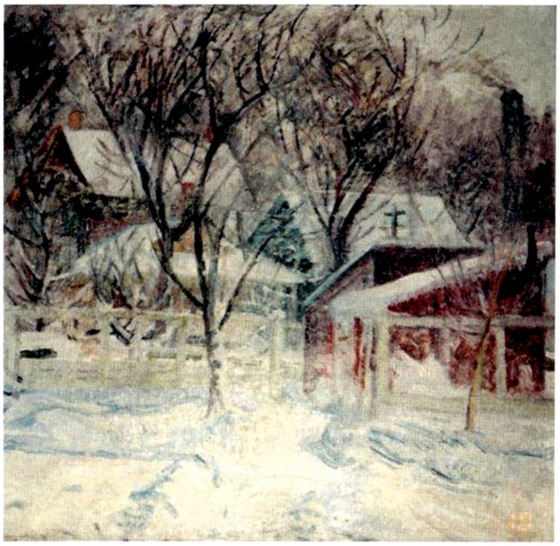

Fig. 66 *Fresh Snow,* ca. 1929, 23 x 24, oil on canvas.

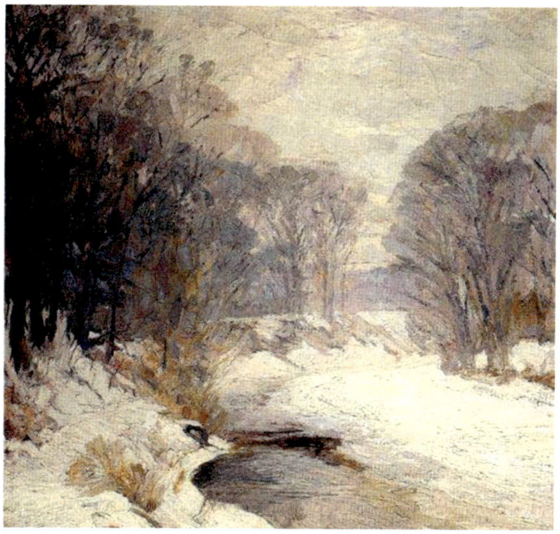

Fig. 69 *Winter Moods,* 1923, 23 x 24, oil on canvas.

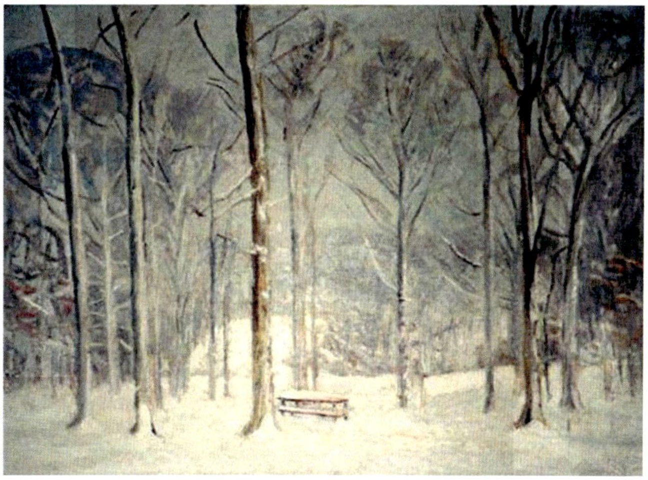

Fig. 67 *Picnic Bench in Winter,* ca. 1938, 22 x 30, oil on canvas.

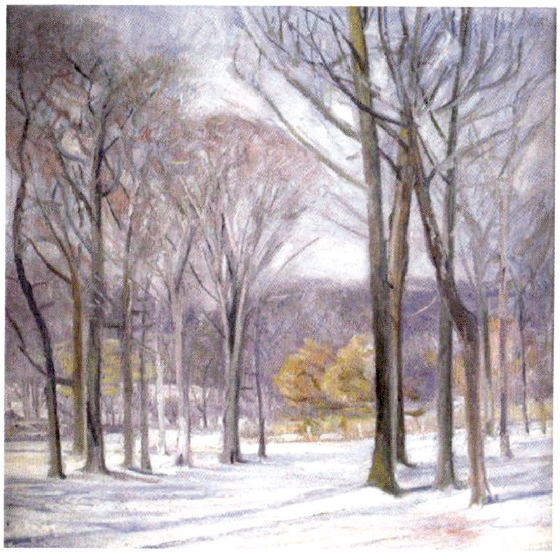

Fig. 70 *Wonders of Winter Color,* ca. 1924, 23 x 24, oil on canvas.

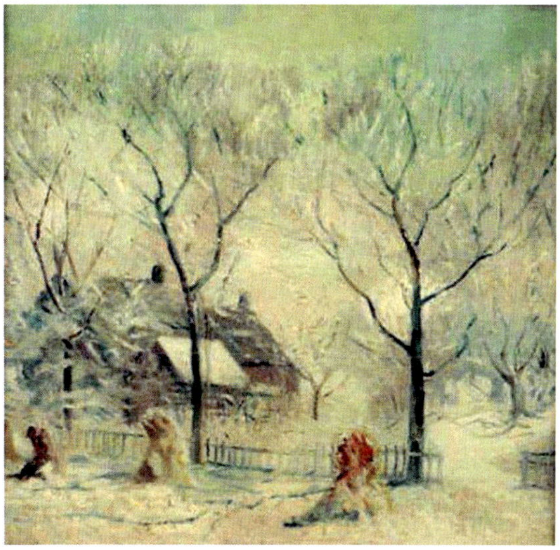

Fig. 68 *Early Morning Zephyr,* 1924, 23 x 24, oil on canvas.

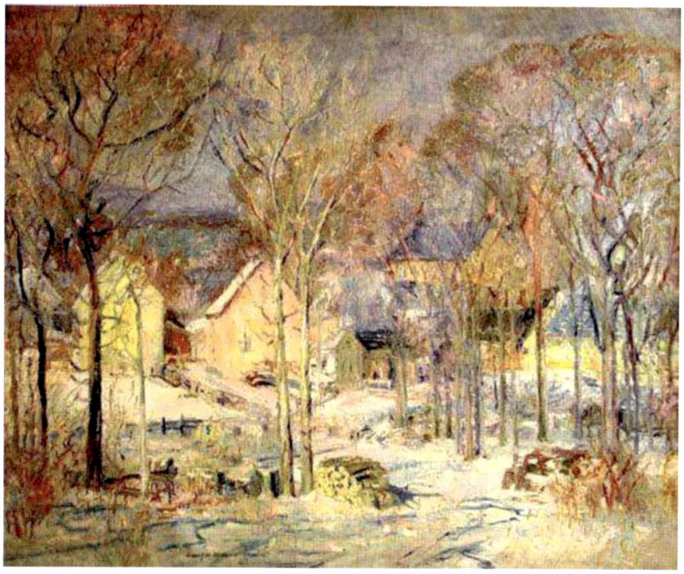

Fig. 71 *February Sunshine,* ca. 1923, 36 x 44, oil on canvas.

Illinois Works Figs. 72 through 83

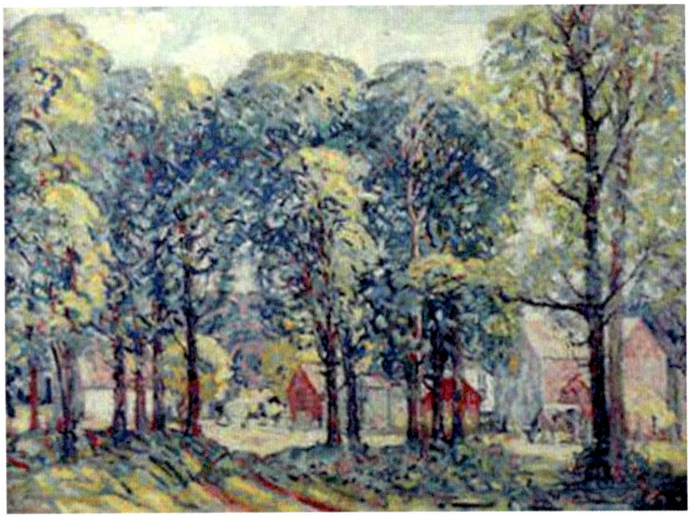

Fig. 72 *Rural Landscape,* 1912, 22 x 30, oil on canvas.

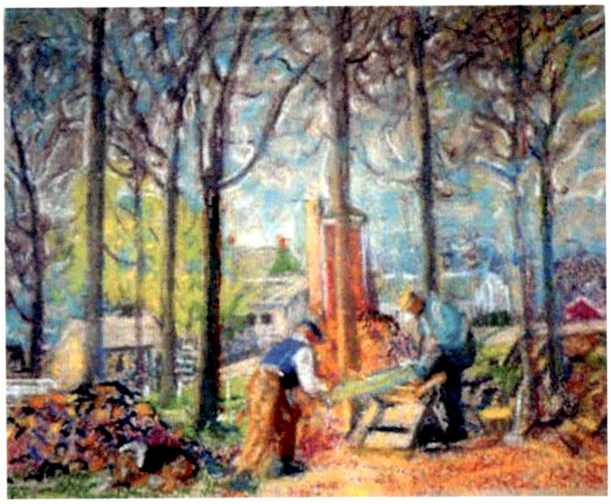

Fig. 73 *Men Sawing,* ca. 1914, 14 x 18, pastel on paper.

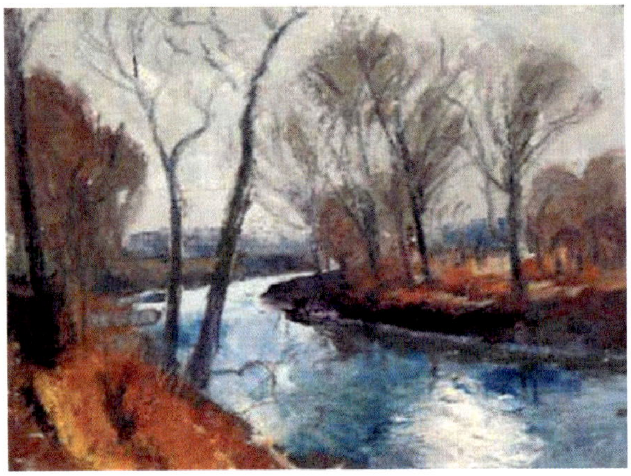

Fig. 74 *Des Plaines River in March,* ca. 1937, 10 x 12, oil on canvas.

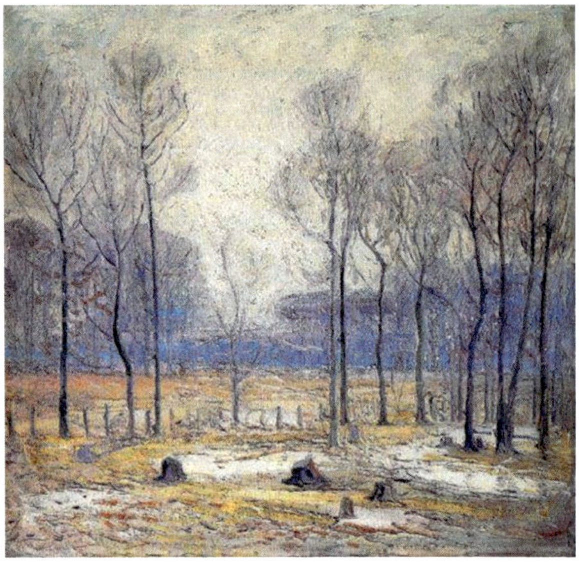

Fig. 75 *Memories of Autumn*, ca. 1935, 23 x 24, oil on canvas.

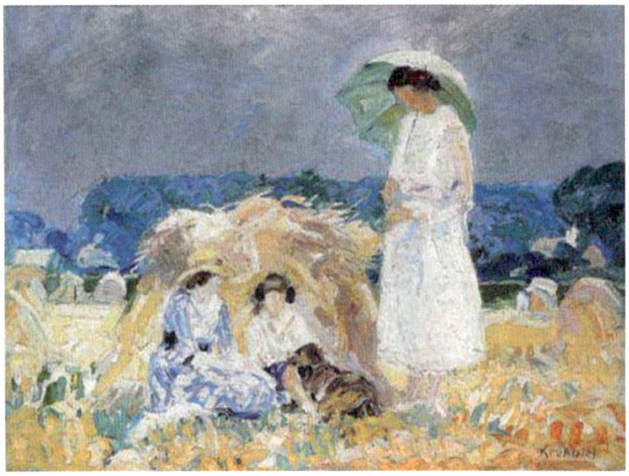

Fig. 76 *Standing Figure with White Parasol*, ca. 1920, 14 x 17, oil on canvas.

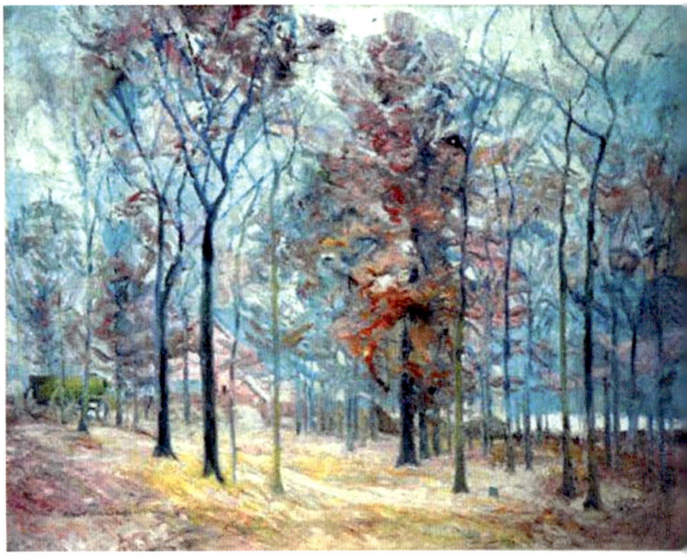

Fig. 77 *Autumn Woods, November*, ca. 1929, 27 x 34, oil on canvas.

Illinois Works (continued)

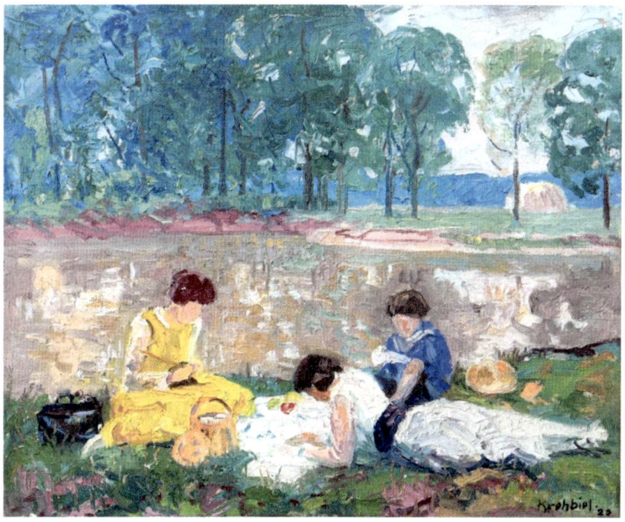

Fig. 78 *Three Figures Beside a Brook,* Park Ridge, Illinois, 1920, 14 x 17, oil on canvas.

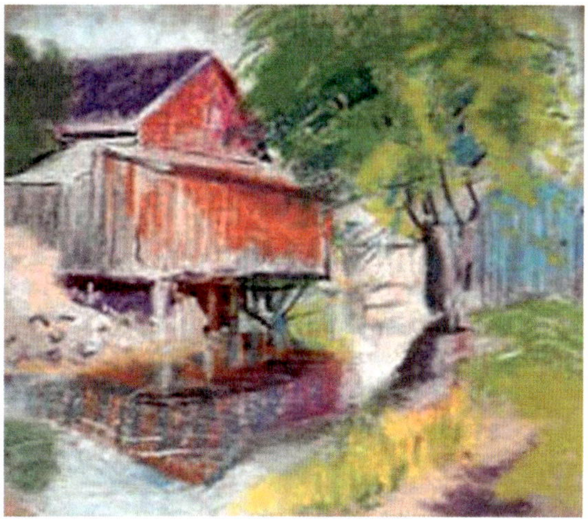

Fig. 79 *A Water Wheel,* 9 x 10, ca. 1926, oil on canvas.

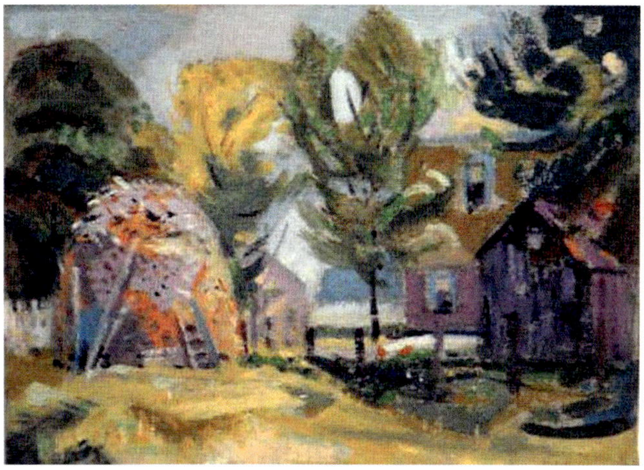

Fig. 80 *Edgebrook, Sept. 21, 1926*, Edgebrook, Illinois, 9 x 11, pastel on paper.

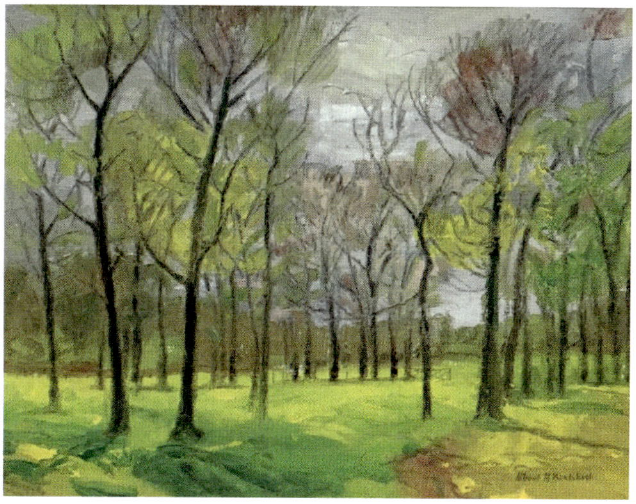

Fig. 81 *Summer Landscape*, ca. 1929, 10 x 12, oil on canvas.

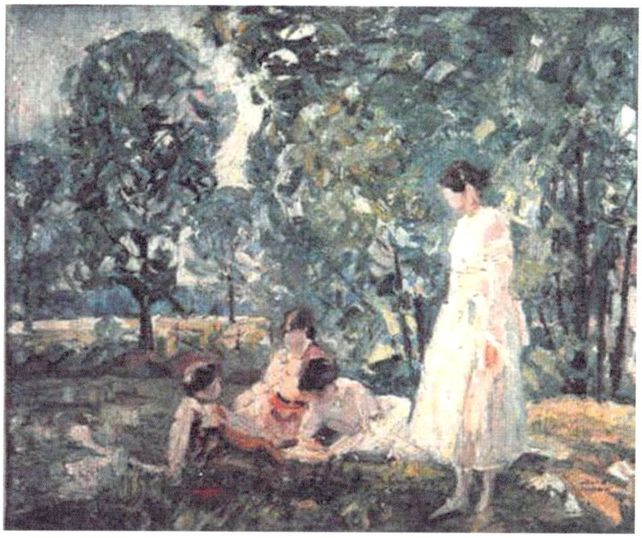

Fig. 82 *Standing Figure*, ca. 1922, 14 x 17, oil on canvas.

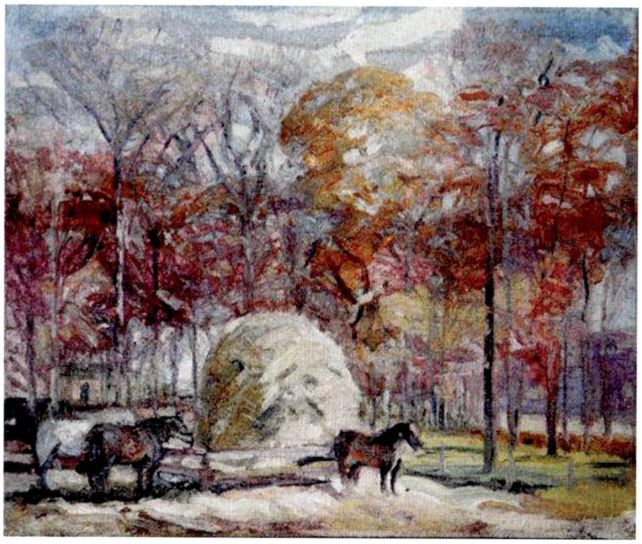

Fig. 83 *Haystack*, ca. 1930. 14 x 17, oil on canvas.

Galena Works
Figs. 84, 85, and 86

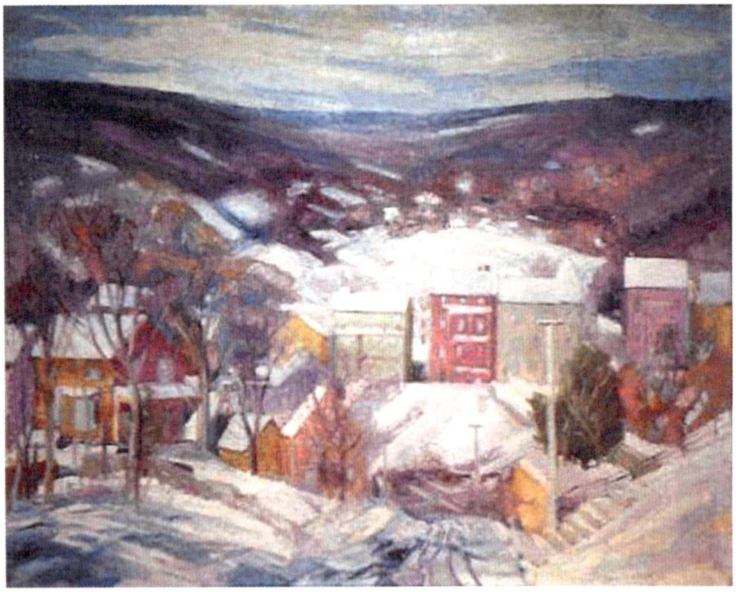

Fig. 84 *Hillside Village,* ca. 1932, 36 x 44, oil on canvas.

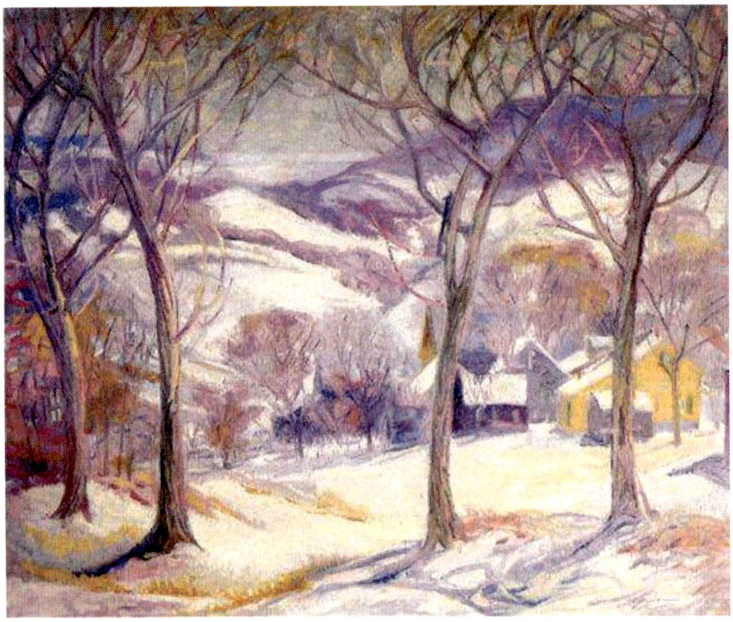

Fig. 85 *Winter Purples,* ca. 1932, 36 x 44, oil on canvas.

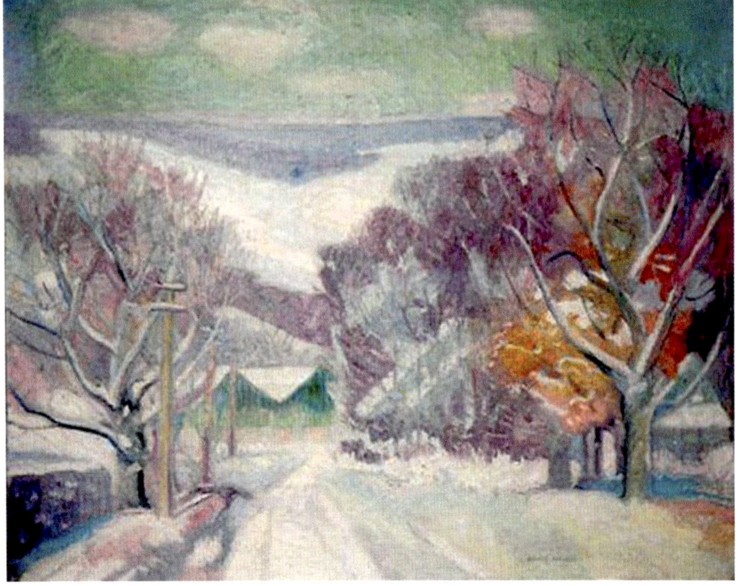

Fig. 86 *Road into Village,* 1932, 36 x 44, oil on canvas.

When teaching and residing (at the Cliff Dwellers club) in downtown Chicago, "Krehbiel turned to recreating the surrounding urban landscapes, most of them within walking distance to his classrooms at The Art Institute of Chicago. These familiar scenes were painted between classes from the banks of the Chicago River and most of them were done during rush hour, when automobiles and pedestrians populated the bridges and streets. Krehbiel was often recognized when out creating his urban works, which motivated him to write some years later:

> ***'I see many things about Chicago that I would like to paint but don't dare to. I'm soon found out and joined by a former student with a paint box, and if I keep it up for any length of time I soon have a class and no tuition.'*** " 1

Krehbiel painted the Michigan Avenue Bridge and the Chicago River numerous times, each from a different perspective. Most of the images of the bridge were executed in 1920, the year of its grand opening, with the bridge towers draped in banners of red, white, and blue ribbons. In *Grand Festival at the Michigan Avenue Bridge (Fig. 87)*, *Michigan Avenue Bridge, Looking South (Fig. 88),* and *Traffic at the Link Bridge – Michigan Avenue (Fig. 89,* ***Chicago Works, Figs. 89 through 94****, on page 29)*, the colors used to depict the buildings in the background – pink, lavender, and pale blue – take into account the effects of diffused light. With *Loading a Freighter (Fig. 90)*, *Workmen by the Chicago River Bend (Fig. 91)*, *Lower Deck Along the River (Fig. 92)* and *El Train Over the Chicago River Bridge (Fig. 93),* solid forms are composed of thick wedges of unblended color laid side-by-side. 1 In *Dusk Over Chicago El Station (Fig. 94)*, the orange and yellow colors implemented to portray the illuminated windows of the buildings and the automobile lights in the early evening traffic actually appear to emanate light from the canvas. Urban cityscapes such as these had become icons of European Impressionism. 1

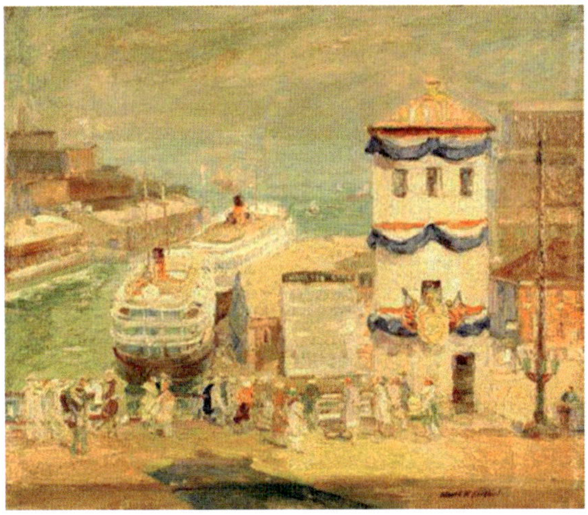

Fig. 87 *Grand Festival at the Michigan Avenue Bridge,* 1920, 18 x 21, oil on canvas.

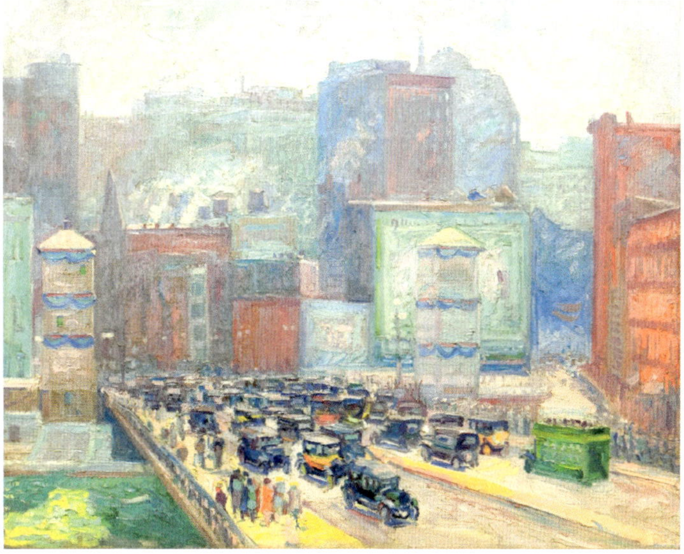

Fig. 88 *Michigan Avenue Bridge, Looking South*, ca.1920, 27 x 34, oil on canvas.

<u>Chicago Works</u> Figs. 89 through 94

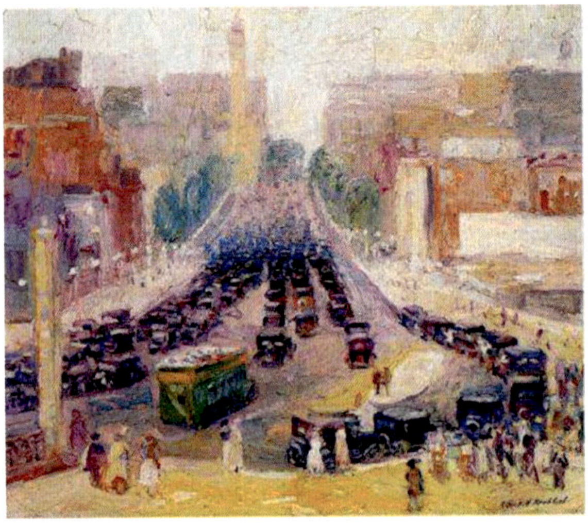

Fig. 89 *Traffic at the Link Bridge - Michigan Avenue,* ca. 1922, 18 x 21, oil on canvas.

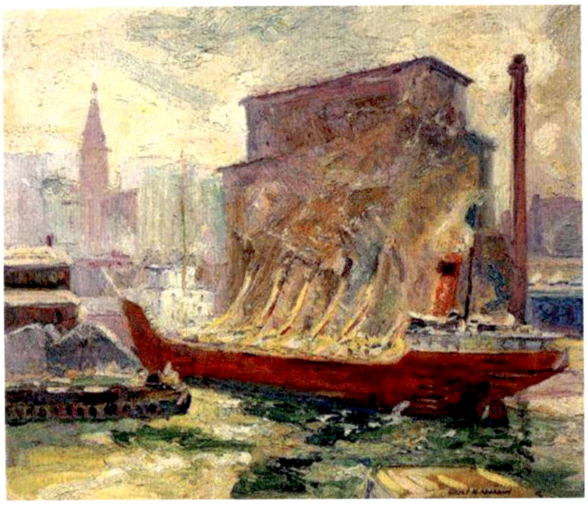

Fig. 90 *Loading a Freighter,* ca. 1922, 18 x 21, oil on canvas.

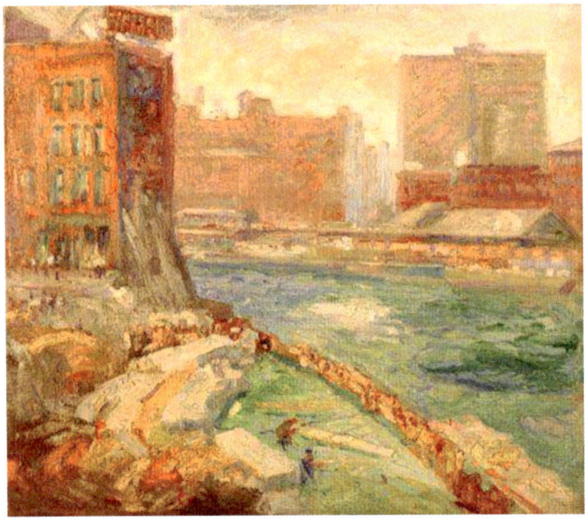

Fig. 91 *Workmen by the Chicago River Bend,* ca. 1925, 18 x 21, oil on canvas.

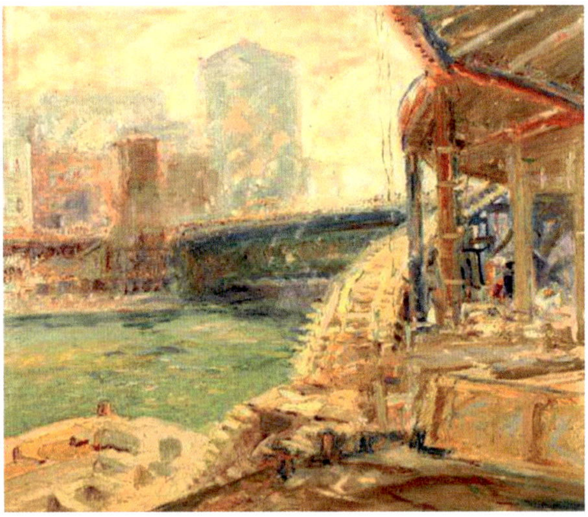

Fig. 92 *Lower Deck Along the River,* ca. 1925, 18 x 21, oil on canvas.

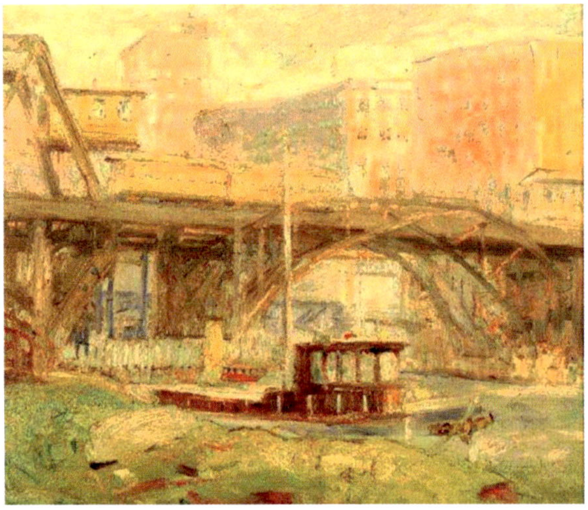

Fig. 93 *El Train over the Chicago River Bridge,* ca. 1925, 18 x 21, oil on canvas.

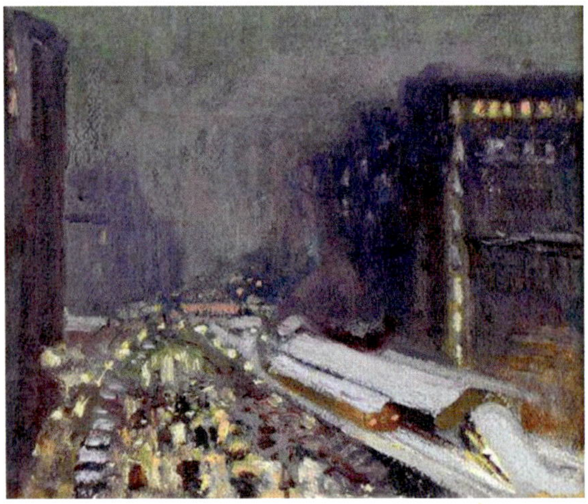

Fig. 94 *Dusk Over Chicago El Station,* November 1926, 12 x 14, oil on board.

In 1928, Krehbiel was requested to paint a life size portrait of Benjamin Franklin to hang in the Hardware Mutual Building in Stevens Point, Wisconsin. Standing a total seven feet tall and titled *Poor Richard*, the historic work was depicted from a small statue of the American icon created by Joseph Siffred Duplessis (1725-1802). The statue was found among the Ben Franklin artifacts collection owned by William A. Mason of Evanston, Illinois. As stated in a feature article from the Chicago Daily Journal, March 12, 1928, the hanging of the painting was accompanied by elaborate dedication ceremonies.

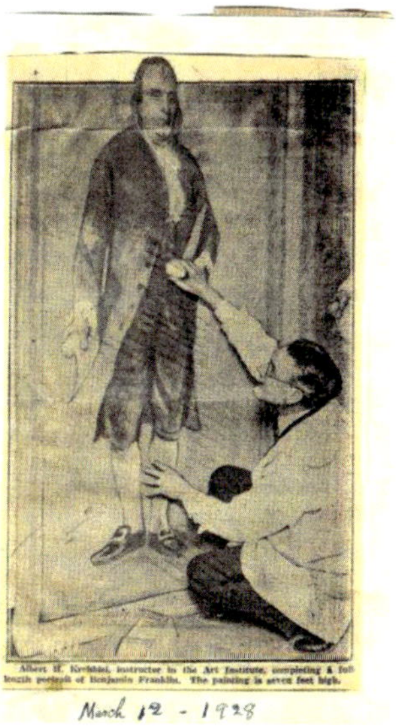

Fig. 95 Krehbiel finishing his portrait of Benjamin Franklin titled *Poor Richard*, oil on canvas. Hung in the Hardware Mutual Building, Stevens Point, Wisconsin, in March of 1928. (Image from a feature article in the Chicago Daily Journal, March 12, 1928.)

Beginning in 1938, Krehbiel embarked on writing his second series of long detailed letters, this time to his son, Evans, who was living in Park Ridge with his mother, Dulah. [1] These letters often describe the exhilaration that he felt when able to spend a sequence of days painting outdoors. In a letter dated December 28th, 1938, in which he describes his Christmas break in Saugatuck, Krehbiel wrote:

> ***"Came over the last night of school*** (at the Art Institute) ***on the midnight bus and started work as soon as I landed. Have gotten my second wind now and can work all day in zero weather and not mind it . . . Yesterday worked all day in a blizzard and did three canvases. When I went to breakfast before dawn, I thought the trees were going to fall, so strong was the wind . . . Worked all Christmas Day. Turned down three invitations to dinner for fear that the light snow would disappear. I have found that a bit of chocolate and a handful of peanuts are hard to beat for an outdoor dinner . . . And to think that I will have to leave all this and go back to another kind of work on New Years Day."*** [2]

In a letter dated January 4th, 1939, Krehbiel wrote to his son from the Cliff Dwellers club:

> ***"Got back the second*** (from Saugatuck) ***but found the institute closed. Had expected night class. It was good to have a day of rest. Like a reactionist who comes back to rest up. I had a good workout, 45 small and large canvases in 15 days. But I'm not telling this to anyone but you. Working from dawn to dark one learns a lot not being interrupted. And at sixty-five one has always to produce something new to show that one's still young enough to grow . . . I am in need of a twenty two-thirty (22 x 30) frame in silver or gold. Any thing that size you can pick up in the studio will do. Can you bring one in and leave it at my locker*** (at the Cliff Dwellers) ***within a week? . . . I may wish to send something to the Chicago show . . ."*** [1]

Increasingly reluctant to return from his painting winter holidays and wondering what kind of reaction he would get if for the first time in nearly forty years, he showed up an hour – or a week – late for class, Krehbiel writes to Evans on one occasion:

> ***"Some day I am going to learn to be real smart . . . to telephone the school on a nice snowy morning that I am ill with a cold, and cannot come down to work. Then go out in the storm and enjoy myself."*** [2]

Synchromistic Works – Abstractionism, a Culmination

Beginning in around 1926 and continuing through the early 1940's, Krehbiel created a series of synchromistic figure compositions in watercolor and in oil on small, unstretched pieces of canvas and, in the latter years, in pastel and in oil on larger canvases as well. 1 *(See **Synchromistic Figure Compositions, Figs. 96 through 100**, and Fig. 101 on page 32.)* The figures in this series reproduce the postures of models in his art classes and, while naturalistic at first, they gradually become geometric, even somewhat cubist. 2 In 1942, Krehbiel wrote in a letter to Evans:

> ***". . . (I) never thought of them as nudes, but simply as a power in organization . . . it became a problem of thrusts and counter thrusts, much like a chess game."*** 2

Synchromistic Figure Compositions
Figs. 96 through 100

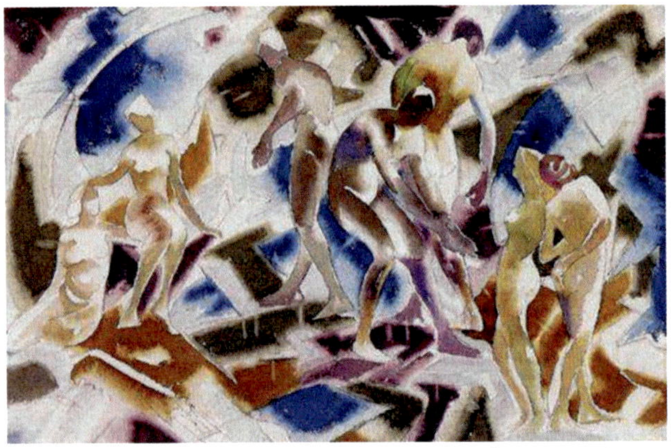

Fig. 96 *Colorful Figures*, ca. 1939, 12 x 18, watercolor.

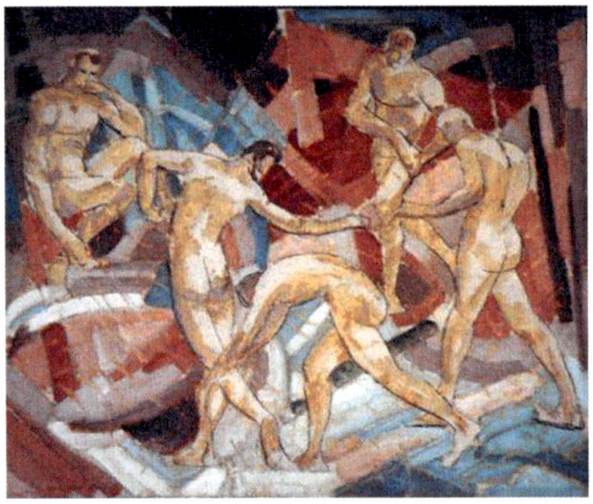

Fig. 97 *Man in Motion*, 1932, 12 x 14, oil on canvas.

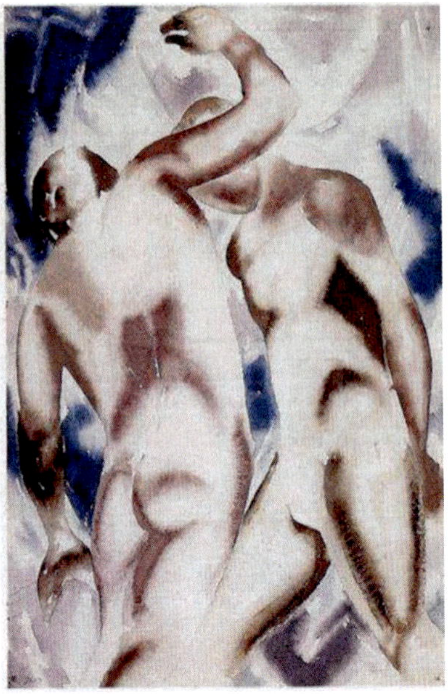

Fig. 98 *Mystical Motion*, 1940, 18 x 12, watercolor.

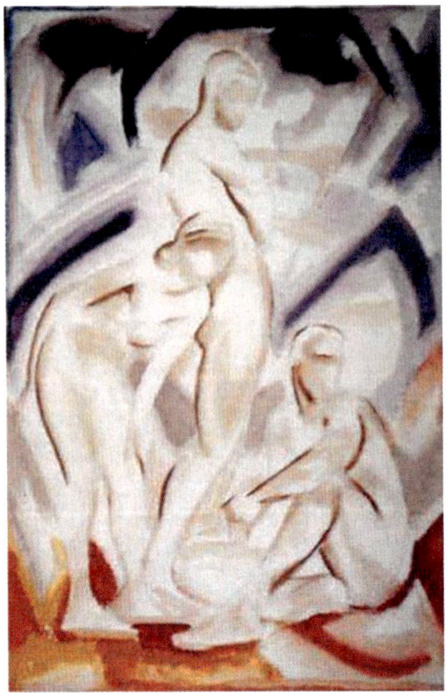

Fig. 99 *Figures on Red*, ca. 1939, 18 x12, watercolor.

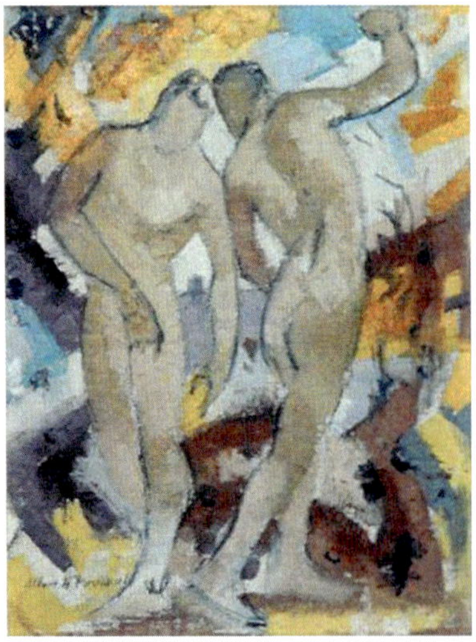

Fig. 100 *Movement*, ca. 1930, 12 x 10, oil on canvas.

Krehbiel developed this new style into a method of teaching figure depiction by having students compose while drawing. Sketches of a three-figure model group, observed from various points in the room, would be rendered on a single sheet of paper – or a series of quick poses by one model would be composed on a single sheet. In regard to this teaching method, Krehbiel writes:

> ***". . .The student should create at the same time he is learning to draw . . .. He has to have ideas to make his drawing count."*** 2

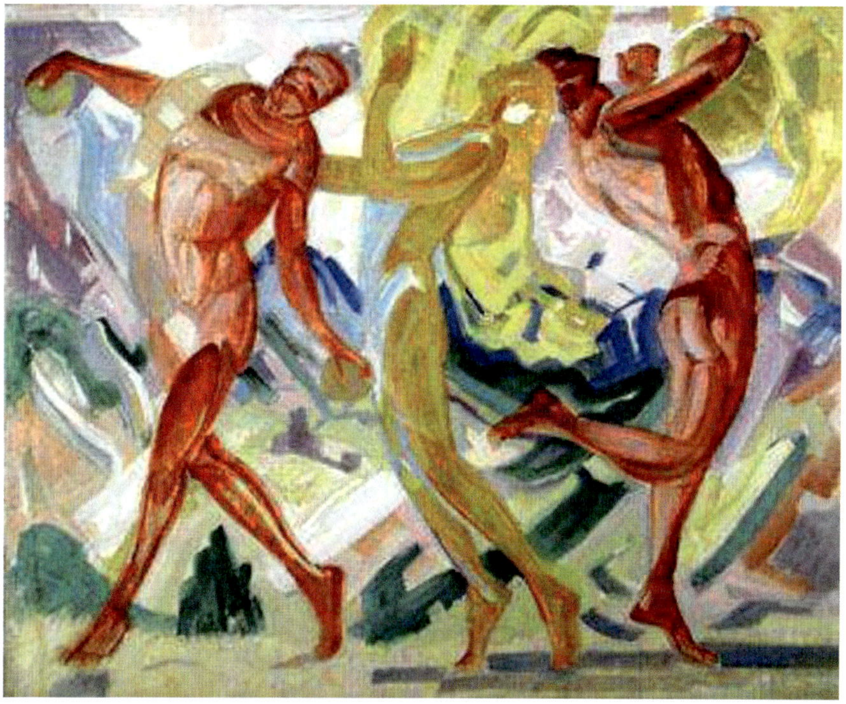

Fig. 101 *Dancing in the Light,* ca. 1938, 36 x 44, oil on canvas.

As for the results of his own efforts along these lines, Krehbiel later speculated that:

> ***" . . . I may be able to peddle them for five or ten apiece when I get out of a job."*** 2

Krehbiel also produced a large number of landscapes in this synchromistic and relatively abstract style beginning in 1926 *(see Fig. 102 and **Synchromistic Landscapes, Figs. 103 through 108**, on page 33)*. Created mainly in Saugatuck, most of these works were done in pastel on paper and were predominantly 9" x 11" and 10" x 12" in size. With most of the pieces, the bright colors seem to emit luminescence and the landscape characteristics come together in sections of singular blended forms.

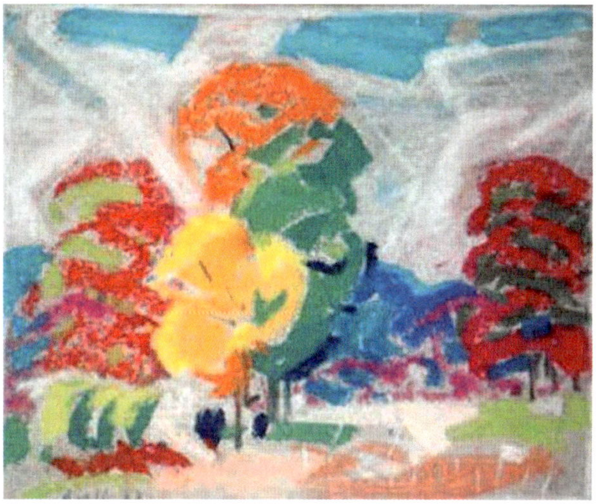

Fig. 102 *August 3, 1933*, 9 x 11, pastel on paper.

Synchomistic Landscapes

Figs. 103 through 108

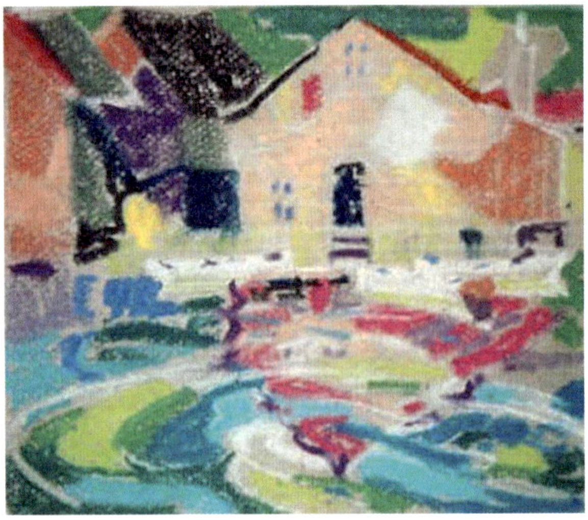

Fig. 103 *July 14, 1928*, Saugatuck, Michigan, 9 x 11, pastel on paper.

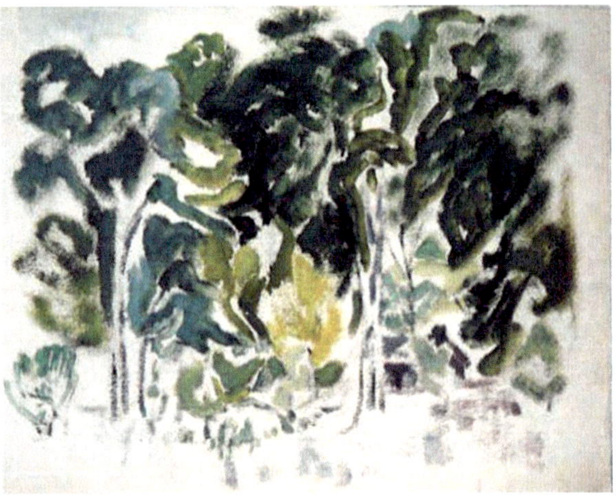

Fig. 104 *Forest Wind,* Saugatuck, Michigan, ca. 1934, 10 x 12, watercolor on paper.

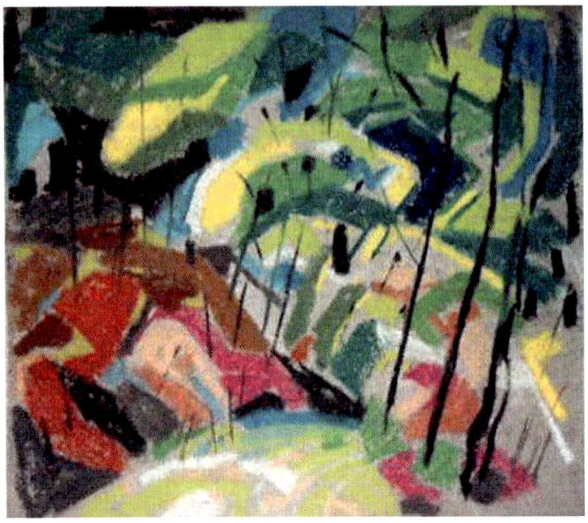

Fig. 105 *Landscape Serenade*, ca. 1930, 9 ½ x 11, pastel on paper.

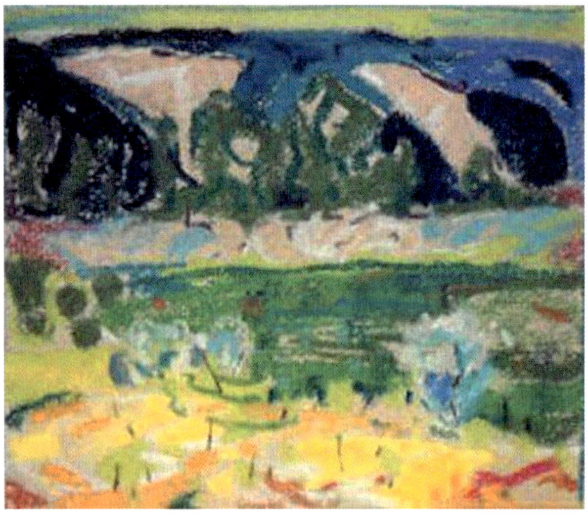

Fig. 106 *Saugatuck, July 14, 1928*, 9 x 10, pastel on paper.

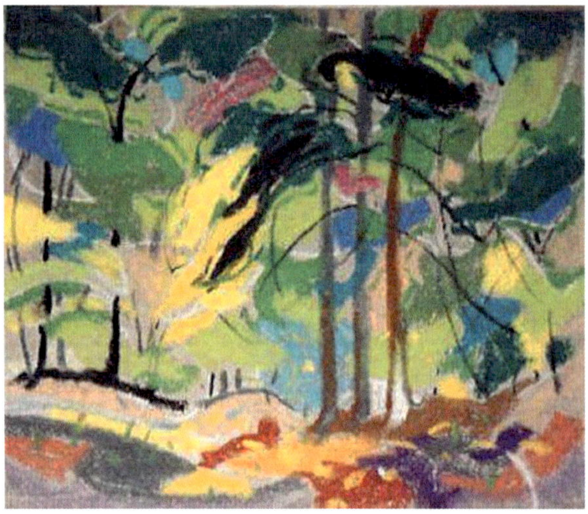

Fig. 107 *Saugatuck, July 10, 1926*, 9 x 10 ½, pastel on paper.

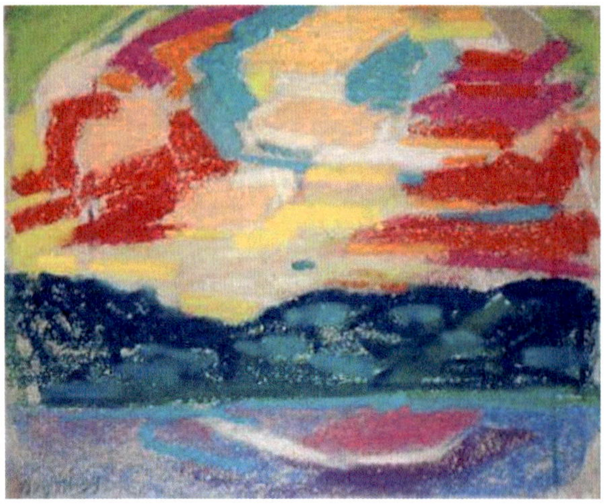

Fig. 108 *Saugatuck, August 9, 1933*, 10 x 12, pastel on paper.

In the early 1940s, Krehbiel created a grouping of very large synchromistic figure compositions on soft-toned paper using pastel, watercolor, and colored chalk -- at times employing a combination of these mediums *(see Figs. 109 and 110)*. Similar in structure to his smaller figure compositions, these works contain throngs of hauntingly composed groups of figures with a mystic quality, sure in line and merged in bold areas of brilliant color. 5

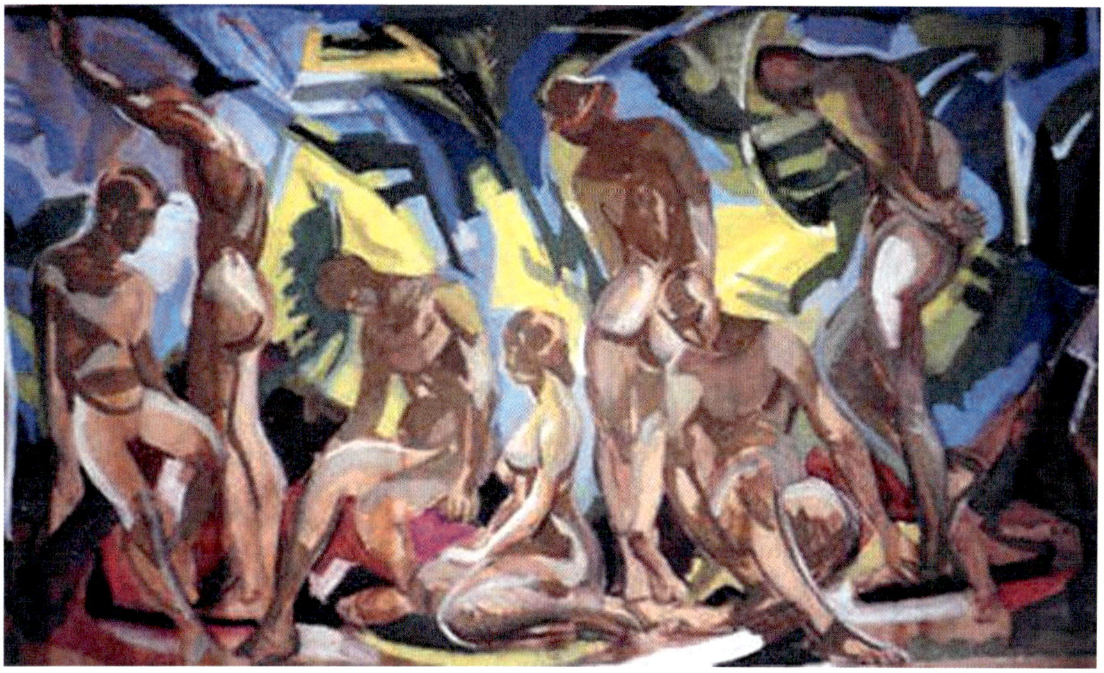

Fig. 109 *Contemplation.* 1941, 46 x 80, watercolor on paper.

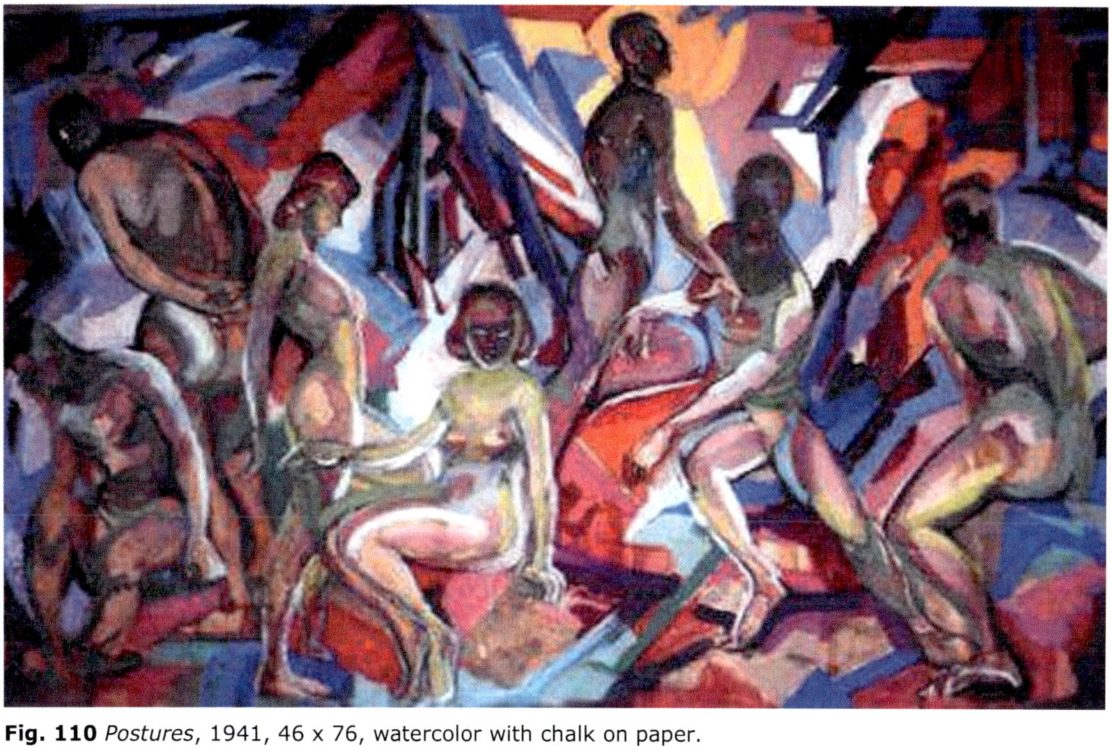

Fig. 110 *Postures*, 1941, 46 x 76, watercolor with chalk on paper.

Inspired by a major exhibition of works by Pablo Picasso at The Art Institute of Chicago in 1940, Krehbiel also drew a number of colorful large abstract studies using chalk on the same type of soft-toned paper *(see Figs. 111 and 112)*. These experimental compositions were amusingly signed "Picasso . . . par AHK" and were largely done for the enjoyment of his fellow members at the Cliff Dwellers club. Conveying his feelings about abstract art and the artist's right and ability to successfully procure its formulation, Krehbiel writes:

> ***"Often I have been asked by my students to start a class outside and teach abstract art but I tell them it is no use, it cannot be taught. It is the sum of a classical education and comes only with the study of a motif when all is boiled down to its very essence."*** 2

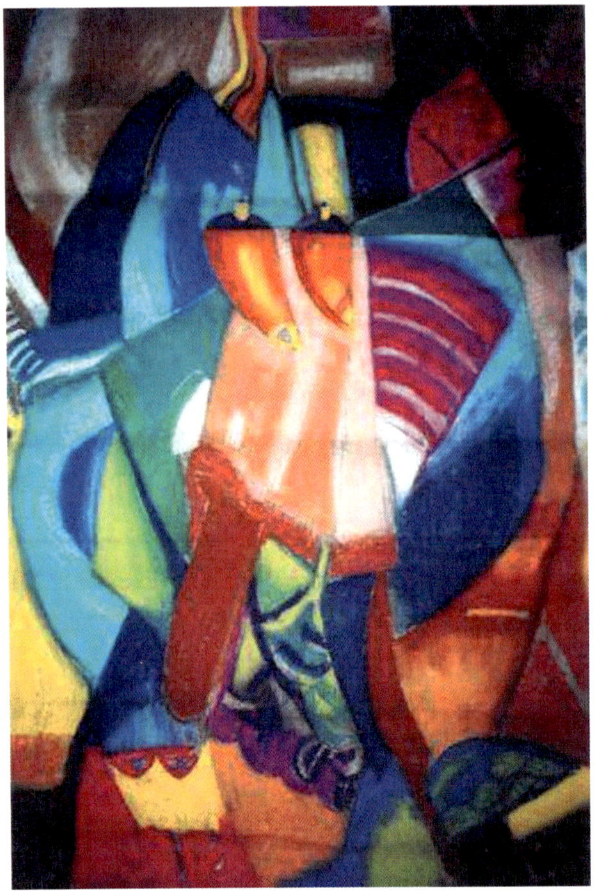

Fig. 111 *Figure Picasso par AHK*, 1940, 54 x 42, chalk on paper. Exhibited at the Cliff Dwellers, Chicago, April 7, 1940.

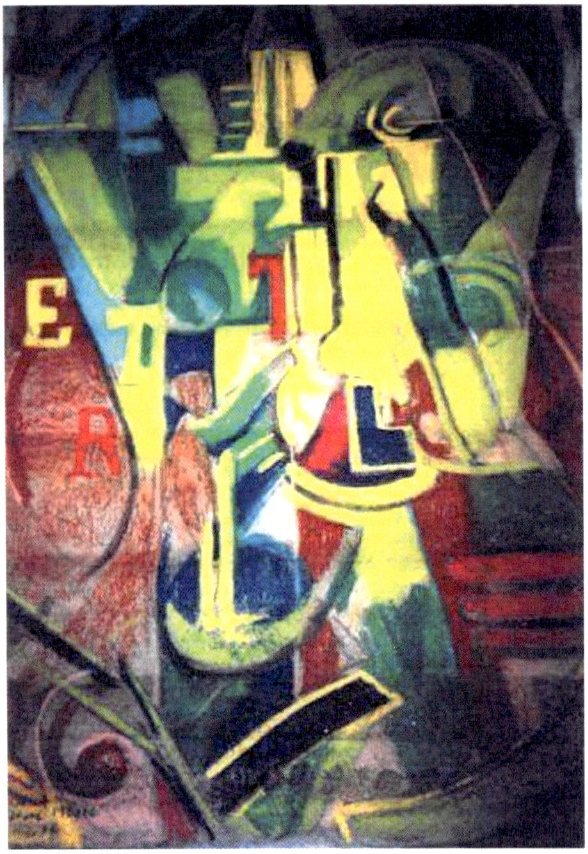

Fig. 112 *Picasso Nature Moiré par AHK*, 1940, 54 x 42, chalk on paper. Exhibited at the Cliff Dwellers, Chicago, April 7, 1940.

Epilogue – Krehbiel's Work Lives On

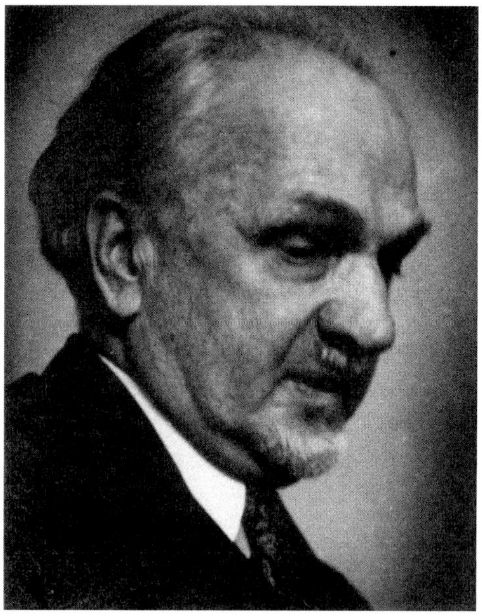

Albert Henry Krehbiel, 1943

Albert Henry Krehbiel passed away from a heart attack on June 29th, 1945, while preparing for a traveling and painting trip through Illinois and Kansas. His death occurred a few days after his retirement from teaching at the Illinois Institute of Technology, although he had agreed to stay on at The Art Institute of Chicago for one more year.

Throughout his life, Krehbiel remained a quiet man who had "little time for the mechanism of commercialism". He had amassed an extensive and extremely diverse collection of work reflecting his contribution to, and interpretation of, the developmental stages of painting and drawing in the first half of the 20th century, leaving behind impressions that take one back to another time and era in history.

During his prolific career, Krehbiel's works were shown in a multitude of exhibitions. In addition to those previously mentioned, Krehbiel's lifetime resume of prominent exhibitions includes the following:

- Two paintings in the Louvre, Paris, France (ca. 1905)
- The Pennsylvania Academy of Fine Arts (in 1923, 1928, and 1931)
- The Fiesta Exhibition of Paintings by Artists of New Mexico at the Museum of New Mexico in Santa Fe (in 1923)
- The First Exhibition of the National Society of Mural Painters at the Buffalo Fine Arts Academy Albright Art Gallery in Buffalo, New York, (in 1925)
- A total of thirty-two exhibitions at The Art Institute of Chicago from 1906 to 1939

Krehbiel was a member of The Cliff Dwellers, Chicago, Illinois, Chicago Painters and Sculptors, Mural Painters of New York, and the Chicago Galleries Association. In addition to his earlier awards for painting, he won the following in exhibitions at The Art Institute of Chicago: the Clyde Carr Prize for Landscape by an American Artist, the Martin B. Cahn Prize for Painting by a Chicago Artist (1922), the American Artists Exhibit of Landscapes Award, the William Ormond Thompson Prize (1919), and the Municipal Art League Prize for Landscapes. In February of 2008, Albert Krehbiel was named the Illinois State Historical Artist for the eleven wall and two ceiling murals that he painted for the Supreme and Appellate Court Rooms of the Illinois Supreme Court Building in Springfield, Illinois (1907-1911).

Many of Krehbiel's works are held in private collections throughout the world as well as in the collections of The Art Institute of Chicago, Fine Arts Museums of San Francisco M. H. de Young Memorial Museum, the DePaul University Art Museum in Chicago, Illinois, the Mary and Leigh Block Museum of Art at Northwestern University in Evanston, Illinois, the University of Michigan Museum of Art in Ann Arbor, the Dubuque Museum of Art in Dubuque, Iowa, the John H. Vanderpoel Art Association in Chicago, Illinois, and The Burlington Northern and Santa Fe Railway Corporation in Fort Worth, Texas. Krehbiel has many works listed in the Smithsonian American Art Museum Inventories of American Painting and Sculpture and writings, personal letters, and selected archival material of Krehbiel's are available on microfilm at the Smithsonian Institution Archives of American Art in Washington, DC, as well as at The Art Institute of Chicago's Ryerson and Burnham Libraries. Books, articles, and writings on Krehbiel are available at fine art libraries throughout the country. Additional information on Krehbiel including books, biographies, museums, exhibitions, galleries, and samplings of his works can be viewed on the Internet at www.KrehbielArt.com and at many other fine art sites throughout the web.

"Happily, there isn't going to be any laying off for me and as my future is still before me, and since things are bound to occur, I'm willing to wager, at this early day, that sometime in the years hence Ill have collected a batch of such sweet and wholesome recollections that can be rated second to none."

Albert H. Krehbiel, Paris, France, 1904

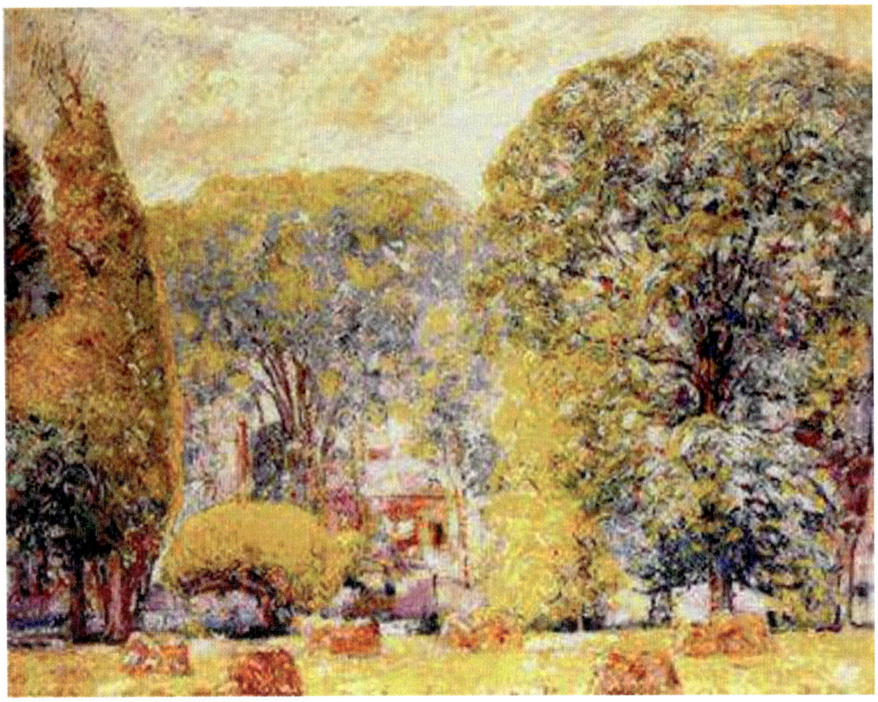

Haystacks, Albert Henry Krehbiel, 1917, 36x44, oil on canvas. Private collection.

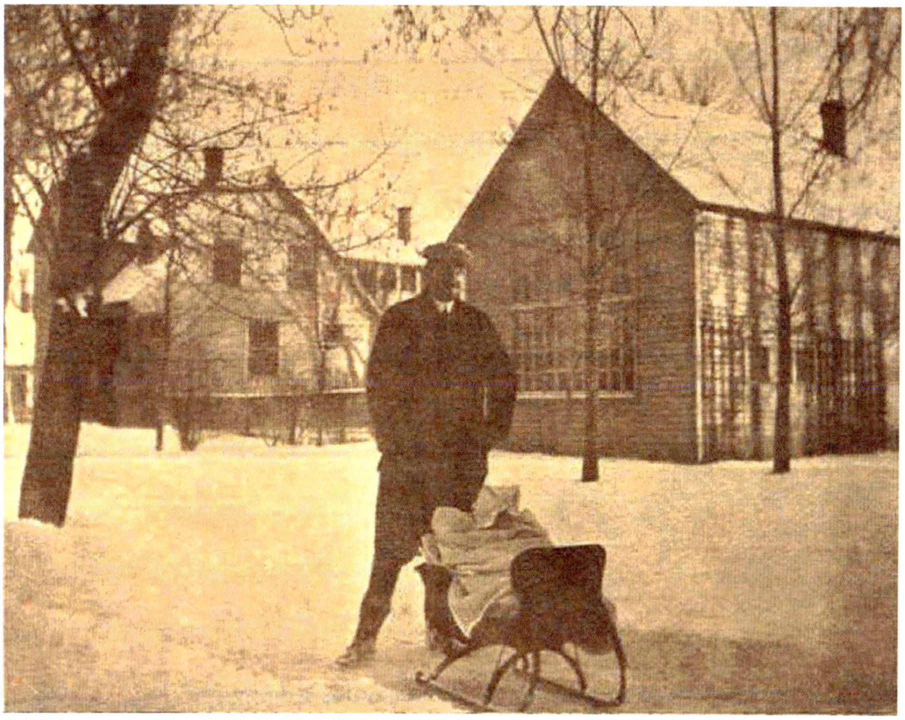

Proud new father Albert Krehbiel in front of his Park Ridge home (left) and studio (right) with his most prized and cherished creation, his baby boy, Evans, 1914.

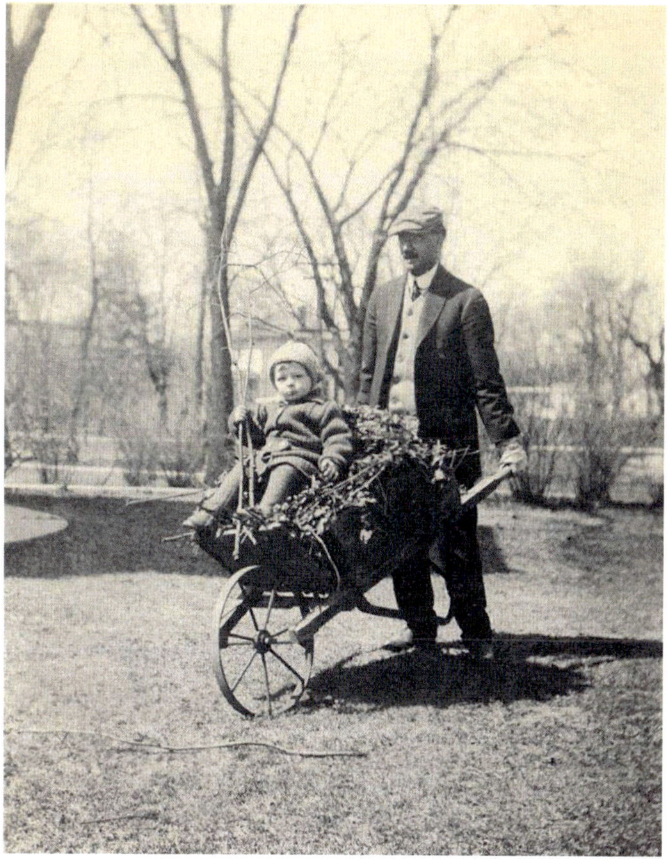

Krehbiel being assisted by Evans with some yard work, Park Ridge, Illinois, April 30, 1916.

Notes

1) ***Albert Krehbiel: An American Impressionist***, by Kim Coventry; Sonnenschien Gallery; Lake Forest College, Lake Forest, Illinois; 1989; 11 pp., ill.

2) ***Krehbiel, Life and Works of an American Artist***, by Robert Guinan; 109 pp., color ill; Regnery Gateway, 1991; ISBN 0-89526-533-8 (acid-free paper)

3) *Allegories of Justice, The Albert H. Krehbiel Murals in the Supreme Court Building of Illinois,* cover article by Lizabeth (Betsy) Wilson; **Journal of the Illinois Historical Society**; ISSN 0019-2287; Spring 1984; pp. 2 -13.

4) ***Albert Krehbiel, Santa Fe Works***, exhibition catalogue by Catherine Whitney; Gerald Peters Gallery, Santa Fe, New Mexico, 1996; 35 pp., color ill.; ISBN 0-935039-93-4.

5) *Albert H. Krehbiel – An Architect's Appreciation,* article in **Illinois Society of Architects, Monthly Bulletin**; October - November 1945; Vol. 30, Nos. 4 - 5.

Sources

Albert H. Krehbiel – An Architect's Appreciation, article in **Illinois Society of Architects,** Monthly Bulletin; October – November 1945; Vol. 30, Nos. 4 – 5.

Albert Henry Krehbiel, 1873-1945; Early American Impressionist, article by Rebecca F. Krehbiel (Mrs. Evans L.) in the **Journal of the Illinois Historical Society**, ISSN 0019-2287, Spring 1984; pp. 14 – 20.

Albert H. Krehbiel, biography compiled for the Krehbiel family by Rebecca F. Krehbiel (Mrs. Evans L.); 1978; 16 pp., illus.

Albert Krehbiel: An American Impressionist, by Kim Coventry; Sonnenschien Gallery; Lake Forest College, Lake Forest, Illinois; 1989; 11 pp., ill.

Albert Krehbiel, Santa Fe Works, exhibition catalogue by Catherine Whitney; Gerald Peters Gallery, Santa Fe, New Mexico; 1996; 35 pp., color ill. ; ISBN 0-935039-93-4.

Allegories of Justice, The Albert H. Krehbiel Murals in the Supreme Court Building of Illinois, cover article by Lizabeth (Betsy) Wilson; **Journal of the Illinois Historical Society**, ISSN 0019-2287, Spring 1984; pp. 2 – 13.

Allegories of Justice, The Albert H. Krehbiel Murals in the Supreme Court Building of Illinois, research paper by Betsy Wilson, University of Illinois at Urbana-Champaign; presented at the Tenth Annual Meeting of the Midwest Art Historical Society, Iowa City, Iowa, April 1st, 1983; 12 pp.

Art Across America, Two Centuries of Regional Painting, 1710 – 1920, by William Gerdts; Volume Two; Abbeville Press, New York; p. 319.

Art and Architecture, section of **El Palacio**, vol. V, No. 13, October 19, 1918, p. 217; published by the Museum of New Mexico and the School of American Research.

Catalog of the First Exhibition of the National Society of Mural Painters, September 25th – October 26th, 1925, p. 7; The Buffalo Fine Arts Academy Allbright Art Gallery, Buffalo, New York.

Sources (continued)

Community Planning, section in **El Palacio**, vol. VIII, No.1 – 2, January 31, 1920, p. 51; published by the Museum of New Mexico and the School of American Research.

Fiesta Exhibition, including the Eleventh Annual Exhibit of Taos Society of Artists, section in **El Palacio**, Vol. XV, No. 6, September 15, 1923, pp. 98 – 99; published by the Museum of New Mexico and the School of American Research.

Krehbiel, Life and Works of an American Artist, by Robert Guinan; Regnery Gateway, Washington, D.C; 1991; 33 pp., [66] pp. of plates: ill. (some col.).

Mural Paintings and Bad Boys, article in **Architectural Record,** January 1908, pp. 77– 78.

The Annual Exhibition Record of the Art Institute of Chicago, 1888 – 1950; Peter Hastings Falk, editor, Andrea Ansell Bien, assistant editor; Sound View Press, 1990; pp. 525 – 526.

The Annual Exhibition Record of the Pennsylvania Academy of Fine Arts, 1914 – 1968. Peter Hastings Falk, editor; 1989; 538 pp.

The court of A. Krehbiel: A niche in the landscape of Illinois art, article by Steve Slack, **Saturday Magazine, The State Journal Register**; September 27, 1980; pp. 8A – 9A; Springfield, Illinois.

The letters and writings of Albert Henry Krehbiel held in the archives of the Krehbiel Corporation, Evanston, Illinois. These letters and writings as well as further archival material on Krehbiel are available on microfilm at the Smithsonian Institution Archives of American Art in Washington, DC, and at The Art Institute of Chicago's Reyerson and Burnham Libraries.

"It seems to me that a good deal has been crowded into my life and I almost feel that if I had to 'lay off' I could easily live on the fond recollections of the past ......I'm almost willing to wager, at this early day, that sometime in the years hence I'll have collected a batch of such sweet and wholesome recollections that can be rated second to none. But best of all, there will be something besides a batch of recollections. For I believe that work with a capital W is the great source of contentment and pleasure, and since consistent work is bound, in my line, to produce something lasting, I hope some day to give pleasure to others in helping them to fish up some pleasant recollection that had most slipped away in the past."

Albert H Krehbiel

Paris, France, 1904

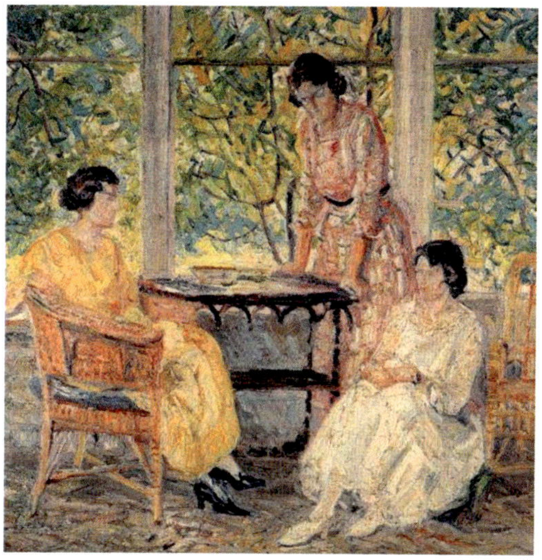

Three Ladies Visiting at Window Table, Park Ridge, Illinois, 1918, 23 x 24, oil on canvas.

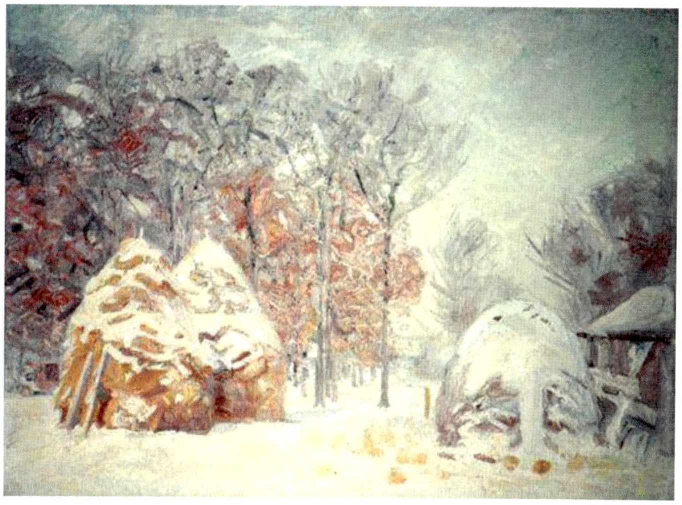

Lacy Snow Covered Winter Haystacks, Park Ridge, Illinois, 1930, 22 x 30, oil on canvas.

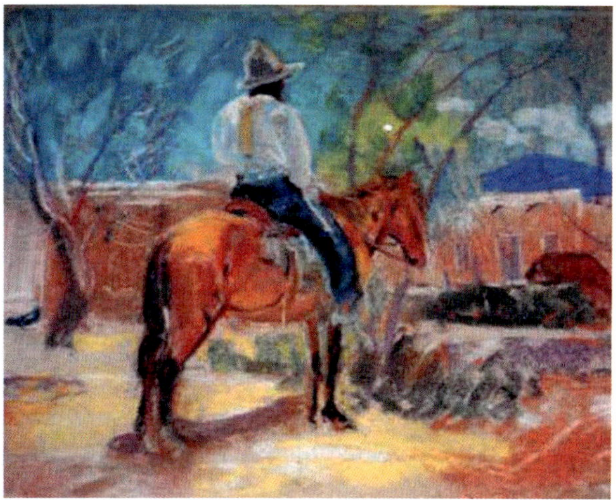

Late Afternoon Ride, Santa Fe, New Mexico, ca. 1923, 14 x 17 ½, pastel on paper.

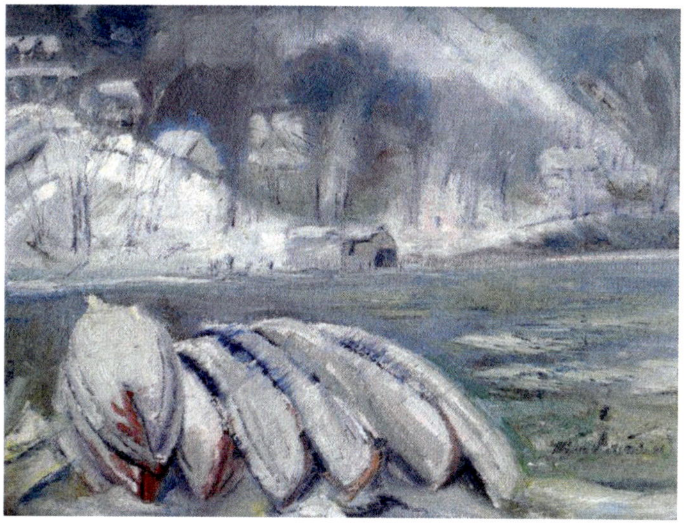

Snow Hills. Saugatuck, Michigan, 1938, 22 x 30, oil on canvas.

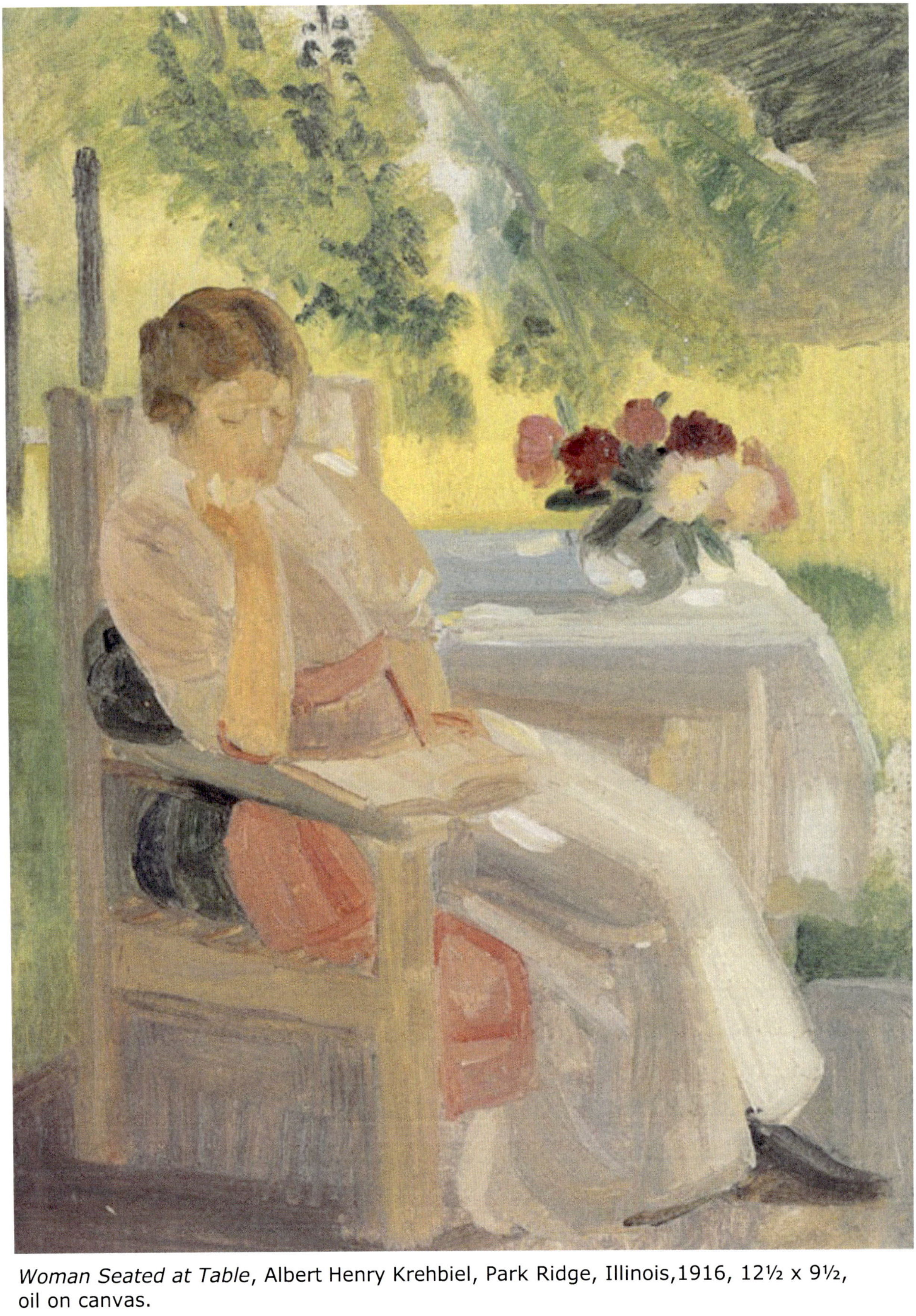

Woman Seated at Table, Albert Henry Krehbiel, Park Ridge, Illinois,1916, 12½ x 9½, oil on canvas.

Made in the USA
Lexington, KY
02 November 2019

56490235R00031